Praise for *Stages*

This stunning book articulates the developmental path of becoming fully alive in Jesus. The stages of growth highlight that faith is not a static, one-time and finished event, but a beautiful transformation that we join as we grow in desire. Nancy Kane has captured simply and brilliantly the essence of true maturity that is neither tedious nor dull, but life-giving and breathtaking. Nancy is the real deal—a woman of vast integrity and depth of passion and heart. She has not merely written a great book. She has lived what she writes. This beautiful book will help restore joy and invigorate your passion for what truly matters in life.

DAN B. ALLENDER
Professor of Counseling Psychology
Founding President, The Seattle School of Theology and Psychology

Too many Christian traditions emphasize a person's conversion to Christ and their eternal life with Him, but provide little vision for the vital years in between. Drawing from the wisdom of Scripture and the experience of faithful Christians who've walked the path ahead of us, Nancy Kane's book is an important and useful guide for the stages of growth for all who desire a life with Christ.

SKYE JETHANI
Author of WithGodDaily.com and cohost of the Holy Post Podcast

When a child is born, the good news we share with others usually includes details about the newborn's size and weight. It's not that we are obsessed with statistics but because we are interested in growth. Life means growth. What is true of the body is also true of the soul. What does the soul's growth look like and how does it happen? In *Stages of the Soul*, Nancy Kane answers this question with wisdom drawn from Scripture and years of rich experience helping others explore the state of their soul. I can think of few people better equipped to lead you on such a journey.

JOHN KOESSLER
Author of *Practicing the Present* and *The Radical Pursuit of Rest*

With wisdom and grace, Nancy Kane offers a hopeful and profoundly practical guide for understanding what transformation in Christ looks like. This book is an invitation to say yes to the love of God in ever deepening ways and to respond to the One who first loved us by living a cruciform life. No matter where you find yourself in the spiritual journey, there is much to ponder and savor here.

SHARON GARLOUGH BROWN
Author of the Sensible Shoes series and *Shades of Light*

No matter where we are in our relationship with God, there is always something more for us. "What's next?" is the invitation of this beautiful book by Nancy Kane. There is an open invitation to find deeper joy and freedom in Jesus, and Nancy artfully shows us how to take the next step, no matter where we are. Pointing out the costs and the blessings of responding to God's invitation to a life of love while practically guiding us toward action, Nancy has crafted a powerful book for spiritual formation and personal transformation. I imagine there will be many in the world to come who will have a rich word of thanks for Nancy's *Stages of the Soul*.

R. YORK MOORE
National Director, Catalytic Partnerships
National Evangelist, Intervarsity Christian Fellowship
Author of *Do Something Beautiful: The Story of Everything and a Guide to Your Place in It*

Stages of the Soul not only captures our contemporary sensitivity for personal "stories," it takes stories to another level by seeking to redeem them. Nancy Kane offers helpful insights into the way spiritual formation actually honors the complexities of our faith journeys.

ANDREW J. SCHMUTZER
Professor of Biblical Studies, Moody Bible Institute
Author of *Between Pain and Grace: A Biblical Theology of Suffering*

In *Stages of the Soul*, Nancy Kane gently but explicitly invites us to say "yes" to God's invitation for a spiritual journey that leads to the intended transformation and depth for an intimate relationship with our Creator. With scholarly expertise, humility and through personal narratives, she helps the reader see and understand the loving invitation we all long for. Nancy beautifully and effectively uses Scripture and writings from several Christian writers through the centuries to explain the importance of suffering and surrender in this journey. Although, we try to avoid suffering and surrender, we learn through this book the transformative role of these in our spiritual journey with Christ. As she often states, "to enter into a life with Christ is no small thing." She addresses some common ways of thinking about and practicing the Christian life but clearly explains how those may not always bring about a real and transformational relationship with Jesus Christ. The five stages presented are not formulaic but are clearly presented in ways to cultivate a greater and deeper intimacy with God if the reader is willing to say yes. I recommend this book to those who desire a deeper and more authentic relationship with God.

NADINE C. FOLINO-ROREM
Professor of Biology, Wheaton College

Rich in both biblical wisdom and stories of people, *Stages of the Soul* reminds us on virtually every page that spiritual formation is a love affair: divine love wants to transform us at ever-deepening levels into love—but at every turn we subvert that transformation, hence our suffering. Nancy Kane insightfully highlights the stages of spiritual formation, the obstacles we put up, and how we can be transformed by our suffering. The reflection questions at the end of each chapter are excellent for personal prayer and group discussion. Keep this book close by to ensure progress in your love life!

ALBERT HAASE
Author of *Becoming an Ordinary Mystic: Spirituality for the Rest of Us*

Stages of the Soul provides a wonderful synthesis of the life-long journey of spiritual growth. Whatever stage you are in, Nancy Kane is a wise and compassionate guide who will help you reflect on where you are, overcome key obstacles, and partner with God to grow in love. I highly recommend it for anyone seeking a deeper relationship with God.

TODD W. HALL
Professor of Psychology, Biola University
Coauthor, *Psychology in the Spirit*

As a professor of Christian ministry leadership for forty-two years, I have had the unique privilege to shape both the mind and soul of some of the finest followers of Christ as they answered God's call in their lives. For most of my teaching, that effort has been face-to-face in a classroom. But over the last several years, my teaching has shifted to an entirely online environment. I have found that in the online setting, one can teach ministry content, and even ministry skills. Most challenging though, is to nurture the soul. That is where *Stages of the Soul* fills the bill. I am very excited to use this book with my online students. Each chapter presents an opportunity for learning, reflection, interaction, and spiritual growth around one of the five stages of the soul Nancy Kane has described. Filled with both engaging narrative and deep content, this book offers the head- and heart-level guidance needed for those seeking to walk with the Savior on a lifelong journey of the soul. Additionally, the practical application helps at the end of each chapter provide small group members and online students a basis for dialog as they support each other on their journey. This is an outstanding new work in this critically important field.

GARY BREDFELDT
Director, EdD in Christian Leadership
Liberty University, School of Divinity

STAGES *of* THE SOUL

God's Invitation to Greater Love

NANCY KANE

MOODY PUBLISHERS
CHICAGO

All Scripture quotations, unless otherwise indicated, are taken from the Holy Bible, New International Version®, NIV®. Copyright © 1973, 1978, 1984, 2011 by Biblica, Inc.™ Used by permission of Zondervan. All rights reserved worldwide. www.zondervan.com. The "NIV" and "New International Version" are trademarks registered in the United States Patent and Trademark Office by Biblica, Inc.™

Scripture quotations marked ESV are from The Holy Bible, English Standard Version® (ESV®), copyright © 2001 by Crossway, a publishing ministry of Good News Publishers. Used by permission. All rights reserved.

Scripture quotations marked NLT are taken from the Holy Bible, New Living Translation, copyright © 1996, 2004, 2007 by Tyndale House Foundation. Used by permission of Tyndale House Publishers, Inc., Carol Stream, Illinois 60188. All rights reserved.

All emphasis in Scripture has been added.

Names and details of some stories have been changed to protect the privacy of individuals.

Edited by Amanda Cleary Eastep
Interior and cover design: Erik M. Peterson
Cover illustration of tree copyright © 2016 by johnwoodcock/iStock (518732018). All rights reserved.
Cover pattern texture copyright © 2018 by Andrei Chudinov/Shutterstock (539978467). All rights reserved.

Library of Congress Cataloging-in-Publication Data

Names: Kane, Nancy J., author.
Title: Stages of the soul : God's invitation to greater love / Nancy Kane.
Description: Chicago : Moody Publishers, 2019. | Includes bibliographical references.
Identifiers: LCCN 2018050634 (print) | LCCN 2019007690 (ebook) | ISBN 9780802496522 (ebook) | ISBN 9780802416902
Subjects: LCSH: Spiritual formation. | Faith development.
Classification: LCC BV4511 (ebook) | LCC BV4511 .K348 2019 (print) | DDC 248.4--dc23
LC record available at https://lccn.loc.gov/2018050634

All websites and phone numbers listed herein are accurate at the time of publication but may change in the future or cease to exist. The listing of website references and resources does not imply publisher endorsement of the site's entire contents. Groups and organizations are listed for informational purposes, and listing does not imply publisher endorsement of their activities.

ISBN: 978-0-8024-1690-2

We hope you enjoy this book from Moody Publishers. Our goal is to provide high-quality, thought-provoking books and products that connect truth to your real needs and challenges. For more information on other books and products written and produced from a biblical perspective, go to www.moodypublishers.com or write to:

Moody Publishers
820 N. LaSalle Boulevard
Chicago, IL 60610

3 5 7 9 10 8 6 4 2

Printed in the United States of America

To my husband, Ray—
You are my "true north" in this grand adventure of life.

CONTENTS

FOREWORD

Consider the gift of years God grants us for the living of our lives with Him. We don't know how many years we will receive. I have given up trying to figure out the rationale God uses for allocating years to each person. Some folks receive many years. Some receive few. Some shockingly evil people live long and die with a smile on their face. Others receive surprisingly short lives. The length of our gift of years we must leave with God.

Our gift of years unfolds differently for each of us in "this present evil age" (Gal. 1:4). Sometimes as our lives unfold, a beautiful pattern emerges. And sometimes our lives unravel.

What marks your gift of years? Many believers can point to the specific date when they came to know Christ as their Lord and Savior. Others seem to have entered His kingdom slowly, in a long conversion characterized by stops and starts.

Now ask yourself a specific question: "How has my life genuinely changed after I came to know Christ? Am I now able to love God and my neighbor in a manner I previously thought unimaginable?"

Another question comes to mind. If an unseen, objective viewer observed closely how we lived over the past week, month, and year, would our lives—what we have actually done day in and day out—concretely demonstrate the genuineness of our words about God? Or would an impartial judge determine that there is very little gold that backs up the currency of our words?

Many believers seem stuck in their journey with Jesus. Perhaps in a moment of profound honesty, we know this to be true of ourselves. We look in the mirror and acknowledge that we're pretty much the same person we were when we first came to know the Lord.

Elizabeth O'Connor speaks sadly of those who never change: "They are the same at the end of the story as at the beginning. . . . Their lives are rich in outer events, and poor in inner ones. They are the impoverished who are not included in any poverty program. They are the dead who do not know they sleep."

"No, I haven't changed," we may admit as we peer at the face in the mirror. "Same bad habits, same sins, same struggles. I'm stuck. Why? What's going on? Is this normal?"

In *Stages of the Soul*, Nancy Kane responds with a kind, firm "no." "Throughout Scripture, we see that whenever a man or woman truly encountered God, they were changed." Yet how does genuine transformation occur? What are the dynamics of spiritual formation and transformation? "What does this ongoing process look like?" Nancy asks. "How do we grow in holiness and intimacy with God across the span of our whole life?" Good questions.

The general evangelical understanding of spiritual growth has been two-sided: judicial (we have been declared righteous by God) and experiential (we undergo a process of sanctification). The problem seems to be that in actual lived experience and practice, we aren't changing as much as we would like to believe we are. Research indicates that 75 percent of all pastors who have served in the ministry for five years or more would change jobs if they knew another job was available. Divorce rates are higher for evangelicals than the general populace. Rates of pornography use among believers are not statistically different from those who profess no belief in God.

Must things always be this way? Is Christian transformation simply a pipe dream? Happily, no. As Kane writes, "You have picked up this book because on some level you want a deeper, richer relationship with God. You may struggle with doubts about whether or not you are making progress. Or perhaps you are in a time of suffering, and you are not sure where God is in the process."

Evangelicals appear to know what is right, good, honorable, holy, and loving. Yet that knowledge has not penetrated deeply into our hearts. How can what we affirm mentally descend into our hearts, with concrete transformation the glad result? Kane offers a profound analysis of how the soul can be increasingly formed and shaped into the image of Christ, a model of spiritual formation readers will find helpful, encouraging, challenging, and healing. She describes "five Stages of the Soul that develop during our journey with God," offering an understanding of spiritual formation that I believe can dramatically shape the trajectory of our life with God as we live out our gift of years.

> This journey takes time, radical honesty, and examination of our hearts. It will require us to be willing to enter into the unknown territory of our souls—the parts we are afraid of

examining. Daily, it will cost us letting go of everything we hold dear to realize what has eternal value. It will mean being primarily concerned about grieving God's heart in all the decisions we make. It will mean loving God more than anything else and allowing Him to remake us entirely.

Yes, there is a cost involved in spiritual formation. And yes, things will take time. Should we be surprised? A valued mentor once told me, "Chris, spiritual formation is the slowest of all human movements." And, as much as we may wish to deny it, the pattern of spiritual formation is cruciform (cf. Mark 8:34–37). A seed must die in order to blossom.

Yet as Dallas Willard reminds us, the cost of non-discipleship is much higher. "To depart from righteousness is to choose a life of crushing burdens, failures, and disappointments, a life caught in the toils of endless problems that are never resolved. Here is the source of that unending soap opera, that sometimes horror show known as normal human life. The 'cost of discipleship,' though it may take all that we have, is small when compared to the lot of those who don't accept Christ's invitation to part of his company in The Way of life." (From *The Spirit of the Disciplines*.)

Quite frankly, *Stages of the Soul* is one of the best books on spiritual formation—particularly for an evangelical audience—written in the past twenty-five years. Read it slowly, carefully, and receptively. The result, I believe, will be the formation and transformation Jesus continually offers to us.

CHRIS HALL
President, Renovaré

INTRODUCTION

To fall in love with God is the greatest romance; to seek Him the greatest adventure; to find Him the greatest human achievement.

ST. AUGUSTINE OF HIPPO

At eight years old, it was, to me, the safest place in the world—the one-story, white brick church was a temporary respite on Sunday mornings from what I perceived as the challenging world of a grade schooler. I still wonder how I found the courage to walk by myself almost a mile to church every Sunday. I recall getting dressed in my "Sunday clothes," strapping on my Mary Jane shoes, taking a deep breath before I headed out the door and followed the sidewalk that led to the front of the church. I tried to enter the church so no one would notice me. Inevitably, I would be stopped by an adult welcoming me with a big smile. I still wonder, looking back, why no one questioned why I was alone.

Once I had maneuvered through the sea of adults and families and into the sanctuary, I slipped into the hard, freshly polished wooden pews and turned my gaze to the cross at the front of the room. My body settled into a deep sense of relief and peace.

I was the middle child of three, with a sister two years

older and a brother four years younger. My dad traveled Monday through Friday, and my mom stayed at home. But church was the place that felt like home; the place I always belonged. In my tiny eight-year-old soul, I knew that there was a God who loved me and was there for me like no one else could be. Little did I know that was the beginning of a lifelong journey with God in Christ Jesus. Just as my body, mind, and heart would mature, so would my relationship with God.

As I look back, I am amazed at how, in my youth, God instilled a desire in my soul to be in relationship with Him. What I didn't know then, but know now, is that every one of us was created to know the love of God and to share that love with others. But with all the people that profess to be followers of Christ, why isn't the world a more dramatically different place? I believe, as I heard John Stott once say, that it is our failure to actually become what we profess.

Not only that, but research indicates that the Protestant church is in decline. Pastor Ed Stetzer explains: "Overall, the Church's influence on Americans is beginning to fade. A growing number of Americans have given up on God—or at least on organized religion. They have become 'Nones,' a term popularized by Pew Research. And their numbers are growing."[1]

Stetzer continues, "Pew's 2007 Religious Landscape study,[2] which surveyed 35,000 respondents, found that about 16% of Americans claimed no religious affiliation. By 2015, that number had grown to 23%, almost one in four Americans."[3] People are walking away from the Christian faith because they have failed to recognize the truth of Christ making a difference in a confusing and turbulent culture.

The cause of the problem previously stated may lie in the fact that we can know much about God and His Word, yet never really encounter God Himself. Throughout Scripture, we see that whenever a man or woman truly encountered God, they were changed. A. W. Tozer writes:

> *God wills that we should push on into His Presence and live our whole life there* .... At the heart of the Christian message is God Himself waiting for His redeemed children to push in to conscious awareness of His Presence. That type of Christianity which happens now to be the vogue knows this Presence only in theory. It fails to stress the Christian's privilege of present realization. According to its teachings we are in the Presence of God positionally, and nothing is said about the need to experience that Presence actually.... We are satisfied to rest in our *judicial* possessions and for the most part we bother ourselves very little about the absence of personal experience.[4]

At its core, Christian spiritual formation is initiated by God and is the means by which—over our entire lives—our inner hearts and outward behavior are shaped into the image and likeness of Christ, resulting in an increasingly greater love of God and others. Quite simply, Christian spiritual formation is focused on the inner transformation and attitudes of the heart, where our character is formed and our ability to love sacrificially is expanded.

Throughout the history of civilization, we see God inviting people to Himself in life-changing encounters—from Moses being called by God to lead His people out of bondage to the tender moment when Jesus asks the woman caught in adultery, "Who condemns you?" In these pivotal moments, we are awakened to the reality of God's existence and the love that creates a longing for His presence with which nothing can compare.

Yet, what does this ongoing process look like? How do we grow in holiness and intimacy with God across the span of our whole life?

Isaiah 6:1–8 gives us a snapshot of the process of spiritual formation:

> In the year that King Uzziah died, I saw the Lord, high and exalted, seated on a throne; and the train of his robe filled the temple. Above him were seraphim, each with six wings: With two wings they covered their faces, with two they covered their feet, and with two they were flying. And they were calling to one another:
>
> > "Holy, holy, holy is the LORD Almighty;
> > the whole earth is full of his glory."
>
> At the sound of their voices the doorposts and thresholds shook and the temple was filled with smoke.
>
> "Woe to me!" I cried. "I am ruined! For I am a man of unclean lips, and I live among a people of unclean lips, and my eyes have seen the King, the LORD Almighty."
>
> Then one of the seraphim flew to me with a live coal in his hand, which he had taken with tongs from the altar. With it he touched my mouth and said, "See, this has touched your lips; your guilt is taken away and your sin atoned for."
>
> Then I heard the voice of the Lord saying, "Whom shall I send? And who will go for us?"
>
> And I said, "Here am I. Send me!"

First, Isaiah encounters the holiness of God, and seeing his own wickedness, Isaiah is undone. Second, upon his confession, God cleanses Isaiah of his sin as one of the angels places a burning coal against his lips. Third, Isaiah is changed by this cleansing; he now longs for what God desires. He then overhears the Lord saying, "Whom shall I send?" Finally, Isaiah enthusiastically responds that he will serve God.

Here we see the dynamic movement of God's redemption and spiritual transformation. We must recognize who we are apart from God and our utter unholiness in light of His holiness. In that awareness, God brings His forgiveness and renovation of our ruined hearts. We are changed and called out to be His presence to the world.

For the sake of definition, *Christian spiritual formation is the intentional process of God forming your inner life, by the power of the Holy Spirit, into the character of Christ, and leading you to love God with all your heart, soul, mind, and strength and loving your neighbor as yourself.*[5] (Matt. 22:37). It is the transformation of our entire being—heart, soul, body, and mind—that God awakens in order to prepare us to further His kingdom.

This process is no small thing. It is a total reconstruction of our hearts, and necessary, as we often are too easily satisfied with the trivialities of life rather than God Himself. We hunger for God but quickly try to satisfy that hunger with something other than Him. The temporary indulgences of wealth, pleasure, power, and honor[6] never fully quench our thirst for the eternal presence of God. Even Bertrand Russell, a British philosopher and atheist, said: "The centre of me is always and eternally a terrible pain—a curious wild pain—a searching for something beyond what the world contains, something transfigured and infinite. The beatific vision—God."[7]

Sadly, the very thing we desire becomes the thing we fear most. We want God's love yet are afraid of what it will cost us. We want to be fully known yet are afraid of the vulnerability it requires. Left to our own devices, we will never be able to let go of the things that have kept us from fully taking hold of the love of God.

Inevitably in this life—maybe even more so for the believer—suffering is often used by God to help us release the things we so tightly hold on to. Pain heightens our awareness of what we value above God. It exposes what holds us in bondage, as we generally don't recognize the idols we have created and raised in God's place. The executive, at the height of his career, suddenly loses his job and realizes how much he has defined himself and his success by what he does. A woman, fighting a terminal disease, realizes she must trust God not only with her health but also her life. A parent of a wayward child is stunned by the magnitude of her heartache and sees how much more she has poured her love into her son than into her Heavenly Father. It is in these moments, feeling helpless to manage and fix our lives, that we cry out to God.

In his book, *The Problem of Pain*, C. S. Lewis says: "God whispers to us in our pleasures, speaks in our conscience, but shouts in our pain: it is His megaphone to rouse a deaf world."[8] As God allows pain to have its perfect work in us, we move from seeking God for relief to wanting God for all of who He is. We begin to see and know, with every part of our being, that God is for us and with us and loves us as His own.

From the moment I stepped through the church doors as a child and felt the delight of being with God, I was—unwittingly—taking the first step of a lifelong journey with God that would be marked by a growing and deepening understanding of His healing love. Not only that, but I see how He is maturing my love for Him in each stage of the journey of my soul.

This process of growing more in your love of Christ and in your longing for Him is realized in the ongoing work of spiritual formation. You have picked up this book because on some level you want a deeper, richer relationship with God. You may struggle with doubts about whether or not you are making progress. Or perhaps you are in a time of suffering, and you are not sure where God is in the process. You may even wonder if it is possible for you to say, along with the apostle Paul, "I want to know Christ—yes, to know the power of his resurrection and participation in his sufferings, becoming like him in his death, and so, somehow, attaining to the resurrection from the dead" (Phil. 3:10–11).

This book was written for two reasons:

First, to explain the stages and process of the journey toward maturity in the faith through an ever-deepening love of God in Christ Jesus.

Second, to invite you to grow in a love for God that so permeates all aspects of your life that others can't help but be drawn to Christ and changed by Him. More than ever, our world needs to see followers of Christ measured, not only by what they proclaim, but by the degree and depth of the compassion and forgiveness they've developed through their own trials and pain.

We often don't see the meaning and purpose behind our life experiences, especially our suffering. Like the Israelites wandering in circles for forty years, we wonder: Is God with us?

Even if we are assured of His presence, we may then wonder: Are we making any progress in our relationship with Christ? We have the guidance of Scripture, the testimonies of great saints throughout history, and the time-tested knowledge of human development to give us a greater breadth and depth of perspective. From these truths, testimonies, and yes, even limited human knowledge, we can deduce five Stages of the Soul that develop during our journey with God. This book will show you the way to experience, on ever-deepening levels, greater intimacy with God and will provide a reliable map of the journey of your soul with Him.

GROWING TOWARD WHOLENESS, HOLINESS, AND LOVE

A Reliable Map

There are far, far better things
ahead than any we leave behind.

C.S. LEWIS

Life is a pilgrimage—a journey to our eternal destination. For all of us, there is the life we planned, the life we have, and the life that is waiting for us. "We must be willing to get rid of the life we've planned," Joseph Campbell writes, "so as to have the life that is waiting for us."[1] While Joseph Campbell refers to a life of our own making, Jesus invites us to a journey on the path to the "life that is waiting for us"—one that He has destined from eternity, a path marked by freedom in Christ and His unfailing love. His invitation is to leave behind our well-ordered, predictable lives to live an extraordinary life filled with deep meaning and purpose. This sacred way involves entering into a whole new way of seeing and thinking, a whole new manner of moving and relating. Through this process of discovery that we will call the five Stages of the Soul, we discover who we are, our unique place in this world, and the humble honor of knowing and being known by the One who created us.

Like a hiker setting out to walk the trails of the mountains of Colorado, we must have a reliable map of the terrain ahead to help keep us on the right path. It is the same with our spiritual life. To understand the spiraling path of the five Stages of the Soul—from Our First Love (conversion) to deeper, Intimate Love—we need a way to navigate and then assess the growth of our love for God over our entire lives. This process can give us a language for our experience and can assure us that we are not alone in our doubts and struggles.

In the courses I have taught on Christian spiritual formation, I have asked students in the beginning of the course, "How does God actually change us?" Generally, students look bewildered and offer vague responses about prayer, Bible reading, and trials. The students seem confused not only about how God forms us but about what the process of spiritual growth and change looks like.

As a young believer, I was told that a commitment to follow Christ would involve a lifelong journey of living life with Christ and for Christ. At some unknown point, I would come to the journey's end and then enter into my eternal, heavenly home. The process, I was told, was clear: salvation (conversion), sanctification (a very, very long process!), and glorification (seeing Christ face to face in eternity). I was further instructed that God would be transforming me into the image of Christ through the process of sanctification as I chose to obey the directives in His Word and live a life of surrender. I would hopefully end my journey as a follower of Christ reflecting something of the character of Christ.

But what about the days when I wasn't following Christ? What about the seasons of doubt and dryness? What about the days when my heart was cold and rebellious and I wanted nothing to do with God? Had the sanctification process stopped? Or what about the days when all seemed well, from my perspective, and I was faithfully following Christ? Was I actually changing then? If I was being kind to others, did that mean my heart was actually changing or had I just learned to act nice? How did I know, other than gaping flaws in my character, if I was actually *becoming* more like Christ?

To be formed into Christ's image and continue to mature and persevere through trials, we need to understand the stages of growth and change. These Stages of the Soul can serve as markers of where we are in our formation so that by the end of our days we can, with full confidence, know "how wide and long and high and deep is the love of Christ, and to know this love that surpasses knowledge—that you may be filled to the measure of all the fullness of God" (Eph. 3:18b–19).

What will it take to become like Christ? Most of us start with the notion that we first must change. We were told, somewhere along the way, that God would love us *if* we change. But the truth is actually the reverse. God loves us first *so* we will change. What motivates us to grow in our love relationship with God is actually experiencing His love in the depth of our souls—to know God as a lover rather than a rule giver. Real intimacy with God—not only worship, discipleship, or practicing moral uprightness—is a giving of ourselves that mirrors the radical gift of God in Christ. We are called to become whole and holy (Lev. 11:45), which means conformity with a love that is willing to give up everything for others.

This journey takes time, radical honesty, and examination of our hearts. It will require us to be willing to enter into the unknown territory of our souls—the parts we are afraid of examining. Daily, it will cost us letting go of everything we hold dear to realize what has eternal value. It will mean being primarily concerned about grieving God's heart in all the decisions we make. It will mean loving God more than anything else and allowing Him to remake us entirely.

C. S. Lewis vividly describes and compares the process of our soul transformation to the reconstruction of a home. He writes:

> Imagine yourself as a living house. God comes in to rebuild that house. At first, perhaps, you can understand what He is doing. He is getting the drains right and stopping the leaks in the roof and so on: you knew that those jobs needed doing and so you are not surprised. But presently He starts knocking the house about in a way that hurts abominably and does not seem to make any sense. What on earth is He up to? The explanation is that He is building quite a different house from the one you thought of—throwing out a new wing here, putting on an extra floor there, running up towers, making courtyards. You

thought you were going to be made into a decent little cottage: but He is building a palace. He intends to come and live in it Himself.[2]

During this transformation, God is co-creating with each one of us to make something beautiful out of our lives that we never could realize on our own. He does not call us to be wandering travelers on this journey. He calls us to actively participate with Him so that we can become the fulfillment of His divine purposes in this world.

A RELIABLE MAP

The five-stage model presented in this book follows the life of Jesus and integrates truths from the Scriptures as it unfolds the *process* by which a Christian will mature in the faith.

Stage One is *Our First Love—Called into Saving Faith*. In this stage, we are embarking with joy upon the spiritual journey with Jesus Christ as our Redeemer and Savior. We see this in the example of Jesus' calling to Peter to drop his nets and follow Him.

In **Stage Two**, defined as *Obedient Love—Learning the Ways of Godliness*, the believer is trained up in the fundamentals of the faith to live and grow within the body of Christ. After accepting Jesus' invitation, Peter becomes a disciple of his Rabbi, following closely and obediently.

In **Stage Three**, marked by *Persevering Love—Invitation to Intimacy*, the believer is invited into a more in-depth understanding of what it means to surrender, along with developing a sacrificial heart that God shapes and forms for

His purposes. This stage involves a more profound internalization of one's faith and belief and a greater desire for intimacy with Christ. This stage often contains unexpected setbacks and realizations about oneself. For instance, we see Peter deny his beloved Jesus three times: "While the words of denial were being spoken, Peter heard the crow of a rooster ([Luke] 22:60b). At that instant, the Lord turned and looked at Peter ([Luke] 22:61a). One can only imagine the searing pain of conscience that swept over Peter at that moment . . . 'The effect on Peter was shattering.'"[3]

The believer in **Stage Four**, *Sacrificial Love—Living the Kingdom Here and Now*, is mature and steadfast in his reliance upon Christ in order to serve and love others. After Jesus is crucified and resurrected, we see a new Peter emerge. The impetuous, anxious Peter becomes empowered to courageously proclaim the message of Jesus to the Jewish authorities; he is becoming the "rock" upon which Jesus said He would build His church (Matt. 16:18).

In the final stage, **Stage Five**—*Intimate Love—Being Light and Love for the World*, the believer rests assuredly in the presence of Christ and surrenders all to serve Him. This is most notably seen as sacrificial love for Christ and His kingdom, even unto death. We see the apostle Peter and the other disciples encounter the risen Christ at the Galilean seashore, the third time Jesus appears to the disciples after the resurrection. Three times Jesus asks Peter, "Do you love me? . . . then feed my sheep" (John 21:15–17). Peter, now tried and tested, is being invited by Christ to love Him by living not for himself but for the benefit of others. Peter's last season of the journey culminates in giving up his very life for his beloved Rabbi.

Underlying Assumptions of the Stages of the Soul

As we explore these stages in the following chapters, there are some fundamental assumptions and critical elements that are important to keep in mind:

- Jesus is our model of life, character, and conduct; our hearts are formed by Him.
- Each stage builds on the stage preceding it.
- The process is not as linear as it appears but rather more of a spiral. As we continue to grow, we will inevitably be circling back and picking up what has not been thoroughly learned in prior stages.
- Suffering and pain take on different dimensions in each stage as we grow closer to God.
- We will encounter unique obstacles to our growth in each stage that may inhibit us from continuing to mature.

CHARACTERISTICS OF EACH STAGE

Each stage includes a section describing the **characteristics** and concepts unique to that stage. We will identify notable qualities often demonstrated in each stage, and what moving on to the next stage entails.

As with any journey, we will encounter **obstacles** in each stage, including temptations that, depending on our choices, can impede our growth. Until we walk into eternity, we will

STAGES *of* THE SOUL

be confronted with all the aspects of ourselves that are not Christlike, all the idolatrous values and affections that keep our hearts from being fully devoted to Christ.

In the book of Matthew, we see this in the man who wants to follow Jesus but whose father has just died. He asked Jesus if he could first give his father a proper burial. Jesus challenged his priorities by saying, "Follow me, and let the dead bury their own dead" (Matt. 8:21–22). We always have before us the ability to freely choose our way or God's way. God will never override our choices.

In each stage, God allows **suffering** for us throughout the stages to purify us and teach us. Enduring suffering—such as relational difficulties, physical ailments, emotional infirmities due to job loss, divorce, or death of a loved one—can be the most significant means by which we change.

By nature, human beings are pain avoidant and pleasure seeking. God will allow the times where our circumstances are unmanageable and our fear and insecurities rise to the surface to draw us to Him. As we move through the various stages of the soul, we will see how God tenderly uses pain and suffering to encourage us to move to the next stage of transformation. Like a small child receiving a vaccination for the first time, we often are confused about why God is allowing us to experience pain. Just as that child comes to understand the good purpose behind the vaccination as she matures, so we may eventually come to see how God masterfully crafts situations to teach us and to see His goodness in the suffering.

The chart on pages 32–33 provides an overview of the stages and their components.

Quite simply, this is a model of following the pattern of our Rabbi to become like Him in all our ways. It is no small thing to accept Jesus' invitation. For each of us, there will be certain things we will need to leave behind—things our hearts cling to.

An example of this ultimate surrender is seen in the life of William Borden. He could never have predicted the path ahead of him when he chose to follow Christ in his youth. He was an heir to the multimillion dollar Borden Dairy estate and was given an unusual gift upon graduating from high school—to travel around the world. While the average teenager was dealing with peer pressure, grades, and who they were going to date, Borden, with his mentor, was traveling through Asia, Europe, and the Middle East. In all of his rich experiences, he was most deeply moved by the poverty and inequity he observed. A passion grew within him to do what he could to bring God's love and hope to the least and the lost. "When I look ahead a few years it seems as though the only thing to do is prepare for the foreign [mission] field," Borden announced in a letter to his parents. His father discounted his desire stating, "Wait until you are 21 before making any life decisions."[4]

In the back of his Bible, Borden wrote his own response: "No reserves."[5]

Borden returned home and attended Yale. During his time there, he initiated and organized Bible studies and prayer groups. By the time he graduated, 1,000 of the 1,300 students were attending the weekly Bible studies.[6]

STAGES	STAGE ONE	STAGE TWO
	Our First Love— *Called into Saving Faith*	Obedient Love— *Learning the Ways of Godliness*
Key Scripture	"This is real love—not that we loved God, but that he loved us and sent his Son as a sacrifice to take away our sins. (1 John 4:10 NLT)	"For this very reason, make every effort to add to your faith goodness; and to goodness, knowledge; and to knowledge, self-control; and to self-control, perseverance; and to perseverance, godliness; and to godliness, mutual affection; and to mutual affection, love. For if you possess these qualities in increasing measure, they will keep you from being ineffective and unproductive in your knowledge of our Lord Jesus Christ." (2 Peter 1:5–8)
Key Characteristics of the Transformational Process Into Christ-likeness	We have an encounter with God's love that leads us to salvation.	We allow God's love to bring our behavior, attitudes and desires into conformity with Christ.
Key Obstacles to the Transformational Process into Christ-likeness	We are tempted to refuse to relinquish control of our life.	We are tempted toward legalism and living a life of faith in our own resources. Doing acts of service and ministry for the approval of others rather than God.
Suffering	We perceive we suffer as a result of consequences of our own sin.	We perceive we suffer to receive training in righteousness and godly living.
Movement to Next Stage	Hunger for knowledge about God and life with God.	Coming to the end of our striving to please God by our works.

STAGE THREE	STAGE FOUR	STAGE FIVE
Persevering Love— *Invitation to Intimacy*	Sacrificial Love— *Living the Kingdom Here and Now*	Intimate Love— *Being Light and Love for the World*
"One thing I ask from the Lord, this only do I seek: that I may dwell in the house of the Lord all the days of my life, to gaze on the beauty of the Lord and to seek him in his temple." (Psalm 27:4)	"I pray that out of his glorious riches he may strengthen you with power through his Spirit in your inner being, so that Christ may dwell in your hearts through faith. And I pray that you, being rooted and established in love, may have power, together with all the Lord's holy people, to grasp how wide and long and high and deep is the love of Christ, and to know this love that surpasses knowledge—that you may be filled to the measure of all the fullness of God." (Eph. 3:16–19)	"But whatever were gains to me I now consider loss for the sake of Christ . . . and participation in his sufferings, becoming like him in his death, and so, somehow, attaining to the resurrection from the dead." (Phil. 3:7–11)
We find, through total surrender, that God's intimate love alone satisfies our deepest longings, and we learn to dwell with Him.	We love God by offering ourselves to Him and the world compassionately and redemptively.	We are completely abandoned to God in divine union.
We are tempted to refuse to surrender idols and deep attachments of the heart.	We are tempted toward feeling self-righteousness that we are set apart by God.	We may find others misunderstanding us and struggle with loneliness.
We perceive we suffer to be purified of our motivations and pride.	We suffer to show Christ's glory and power.	We share in Christ's sufferings.
Coming to a profound sense of our identity in Christ; ego attachments have fallen away; content in abiding in Christ.	Coming to a realization of a deep sense of union with Christ.	Coming into a deeper realization of the thin veil between eternity and the present moment.

Beyond campus, Borden was involved in the local mission in New Haven, caring for those in need. To help people he found on the streets struggling with alcoholism, he founded a not-for-profit to assist them in recovery.[7]

After graduating from Yale, Borden followed his growing conviction to minister to people of the Muslim faith in China.[8] He attended and graduated from Princeton Seminary and then joined the China Inland Mission. At that time, it is said that he wrote two more words in his Bible: "No retreat."

Borden set sail for China and stopped first in Egypt to become proficient in Arabic. While in Egypt, he contracted spinal meningitis. And then, during his illness, with the threat of his life being cut short, it is said he wrote these words in his Bible: "No regrets."

Borden's entry echoes the words of the apostle Paul in his letter to Timothy: "For I am already being poured out like a drink offering, and the time for my departure is near. I have fought the good fight, I have finished the race, I have kept the faith. Now there is in store for me the crown of righteousness, which the Lord, the righteous Judge, will award to me on that day—and not only to me, but also to all who have longed for his appearing" (2 Tim. 4:6–8). Nineteen days later, at the age of twenty-five, William Whiting Borden entered into eternity. His tombstone in Egypt is engraved with these words: "Apart from Christ there is no explanation for such a life."

This is the brief and devoted life of William Borden: *no reserves, no retreat, no regrets.* There is no human way to explain the impact that Borden's life had on others. Borden was captivated by the love of God. He chose the path Jesus referred to as the "narrow road that leads to life" (Matt. 7:14).

May God grant us the courage to follow Him on the path of life. Let the journey begin.

STAGE ONE:
OUR FIRST LOVE
Called into Saving Faith

The needs of the world are too great, the
suffering and pain too extensive, the lures
of the world too seductive for us to begin
to change the world unless we are changed,
unless conversion of life and morals becomes
our pattern. The status quo is too alluring.

WILLIAM WILLIMON

Bread and Wine

In His passion to set in order a shattered and fragmented
world, God broke open His own heart in love. God sent
Jesus Christ into the pain and suffering of this fallen world
so that we might live into the delight of His divine life and
love. The love between God the Father and the Son is now
our invitation to be gathered in the Spirit to share in that
love. He loves us fully and completely in Christ. As Francis
Thompson's poem, "The Hound of Heaven" says,[1] though we

run from Him, God is the unrelenting hound of heaven, pursuing us and inviting us to experience His love, which existed before all other earthly loves.

Henri Nouwen describes this "first love" well:

> The spiritual life starts at the place where you can hear God's voice. Where somehow you can claim that long before your father, your mother, your brother, your sister, your school, your church touched you, loved you and wounded you—long before that, you were held safe in an eternal embrace. You were seen with eyes of perfect love, long before you entered into a dark valley of life . . . The spiritual life starts at the moment you can go beyond all the wounds and claim that there was a love that was perfect and unlimited, long before that perfect love reflected in the imperfect and limited, conditional love of people. The spiritual life starts where you dare to claim the first love.[2]

CHARACTERISTICS OF STAGE ONE

In this first stage of the soul, the encounter with God's perfect love in Jesus Christ is one that invites us to a radical change of mind, heart, body, and soul. God's singular focus is to make us like Jesus Christ and be in relationship with Him. His love is unconditionally offered to us, but there must be a releasing of the rule of our own lives in order to surrender and receive His love.

Nicodemus was a man of excellent moral standing and religious credentials, being a Pharisee and member of the Sanhedrin. He arrived in the cover of night honestly seeking. Nicodemus's fine religious credentials did not impress Jesus nor did the earnest intentions of his heart. Jesus simply tells Nicodemus that he must be "born again," using the metaphor of birth to illustrate that being redeemed is so radical, it is like being born all over again.

We are powerless to save ourselves. Like Paul we affirm, "For I do not understand my own actions. For I do not do what I want, but I do the very thing I hate . . . For I know that nothing good dwells in me, that is, in my flesh. For I have the desire to do what is right, but not the ability to carry it out" (Romans 7:15, 18 ESV).

Jesus came to restore our broken and fragmented souls. He came to heal all the ways that sin has ruined us. In Jesus' inaugural address in the temple, He stood up and read from the book of Isaiah.

> The Spirit of the Lord is upon me,
>   because he has anointed me
>   to proclaim good news to the poor.
> He has sent me to proclaim liberty to the captives
>   and recovering of sight to the blind,
>   to set at liberty those who are oppressed,
> to proclaim the year of the Lord's favor. (Luke 4:18–19 ESV)

As soon as Jesus spoke, people noticed an unusual authority and vibrancy evident in every word. Then the moment came: "Today this scripture is fulfilled in your hearing" (Luke 4:21). The promise of God to His people was realized in the very presence of Jesus.

God flings open the prison doors of sin in our souls that have confined us and invites us to live a life fully in His presence. Tim Keller, author and pastor, describes sin as ". . . looking to something else besides God for your salvation.

It is putting yourself in the place of God, becoming your own savior and lord."[3] Jesus wants to set us free from our own sinful self-rule but also from rejection, abuse, shame, and despair. He invites us into a relationship of intimacy in which we need to let go of our performance mentality by trying to manage our own lives; to let go of our masks and facades; and to lay our sin, wounds, and burdens before Him and allow Him to forgive, heal, and renew us. God the Father adopts us as His sons and daughters to learn to live as He lived and to share His heart (Rom. 5:10; 8:15).

One autumn Sunday in my middle school years, I felt Jesus' call to follow Him. I was enrolled in a confirmation class that was required for young adults prior to seeking church membership. We learned things that at that age most find less than exciting, like the names of the books of the Bible, the Ten Commandments, and the Apostles' Creed. But what kept us coming back each Sunday was our teacher—a middle-aged, chain-smoking man who, it was clear to all of us, was actually excited about teaching us these things about God, His Son, and His church. But one Sunday, the routine and boredom of this class was disrupted. Our beloved teacher led us to the gospels and Jesus' invitation to His disciples and to Peter, "Come, follow me."

Suddenly, I recall, it was as if something came over our teacher, who became even more animated than usual. With a conviction in his voice and tears in his eyes that left us all awestruck, he said, "And now, Jesus invites each one of you. Will you follow Me?" It felt like I was moved out of time and space as though Jesus Himself was in front of me, extending His hand of invitation. If fear of embarrassment hadn't seized control, I would have leaped out of my chair and said, "Yes! Yes, I will follow Him!" I left the church that day with a meaning and purpose for life. I skipped home, singing songs all the way. As I walked, everywhere I looked seemed to express the glory and beauty of God and His creation. It was a turning point for me. All the stories I had learned thus far in the Bible became personal.

That moment, as with all the saints throughout history, God was setting me apart, calling me to follow Him. When this kind of experience happens, the Spirit of God takes residence in our souls (Eph. 1:13). He gently turns the gaze of our soul from ourselves to Himself. But that is only the beginning. He guides us into all truth, intercedes for us before His Father, comforts us in times of pain, and empowers us to become and live like Him. Our hearts overflow with joy for the outrageous love of God. Like newborn infants, we crave the nourishment He can provide. We gladly release what we have cherished and find our hearts satisfied with all that God freely gives us.

St. Augustine eloquently describes his experience of God's lavish love after a lengthy struggle of resisting Him:

> Late have I loved you, O Beauty ever ancient, ever new, late have I loved you! You were within me, but I was outside, and it was there that I searched for you. In my unloveliness I plunged into the lovely things which you created. You were with me, but I was not with you. Created things kept me from you; yet if they had not been in you they would have not been at all. You called, you shouted, and you broke through my deafness.

> You flashed, you shone, and you dispelled my blindness. You
> breathed your fragrance on me; I drew in a breath and now
> I pant for you. I have tasted you, now I hunger and thirst for
> more. You touched me, and I burned for your peace.[4]

God's invitation to this "first love" stage is the foundation of all that follows in the journey of the soul. What was true for Augustine is also true for each one of us. Only God can love us perfectly. We have all grown up in a world where, even though our mothers, fathers, friends, and spouses mean well, they have loved us imperfectly. We have all been disappointed in love. But God, who knew us before He formed us in our mother's womb (Jer. 1:5a), also knew that He could heal our wounded hearts and set us on a new path of being loved sons and daughters of the Creator of the universe.

In so many ways, God is restoring within us the trust and ability to see God's hand in our lives. C. S. Lewis reminds us, "But God will look to every soul like its first love because He is its first love. Your place in heaven will seem to be made for you and you alone, because you were made for it—made for it stitch by stitch as a glove is made for a hand."[5]

The story is told of a young couple who had given birth to a baby boy. Their daughter asked to be alone with her new tiny brother. As the parents listened through the intercom, they heard her say, "Tell me about heaven. I'm beginning to forget."[6] The childlike trust we see in this sweet story is reminiscent of the type of faith evident in this stage . . . a faith that unquestioningly believes but that can also wane, rather than grow deeper, with time. It is in this first stage that we are granted the grace to believe that God's love satisfies our deepest desires and that "heaven" contains what our hearts have always longed for.

This First Love stage is the foundation of our relationship with Christ. Although at times we will need to circle back up the spiraling path to earlier stages and re-acquire a better understanding of the full depth and breadth of God's love, we must keep our eyes set on Christ and our final stage of Intimate Love. As with any journey there will be a need for courage and perseverance. And, as with any journey, there will be unanticipated detours and setbacks.

OBSTACLES TO GROWTH

To enter into a life with Christ is no small thing. Conversion will expose everything we have been following and worshipping instead of Christ. In the well-known interaction between Jesus and the rich man (Matt. 19:16–22), we see a man who was eager to take the next step toward the assurance of eternal life. Jesus instructed him that he must keep the commandments—do not murder, do not commit adultery, do not steal, do not bear false witness, honor one's parents, and love your neighbor as yourself. The rich man was confident that he had perfectly fulfilled all of God's commandments Jesus listed.

But Jesus wisely discerns that the rich man fails to see his preoccupation with wealth. Jesus asks him to first sell everything he possesses. Quite telling in this interaction is that the rich man goes away saddened; he was unwilling to release the riches he held so dear. Instead, the rich man placed his trust in the accumulation of his wealth, and that accumulation left no room in his soul for loving and following Jesus. For many, the possessions, comforts, and even sins of their former life have become strongholds, and they find it easier to go back to the lives they once knew.

Others allow pride to creep in and take hold. They want Christ *and* _____. They want the riches of the new life in Christ, and they want to maintain the esteem of their friends, the security of their social networks, and the power and status that comes with their careers. They are unwilling to keep Christ first. They feel assured of "eternal" life but are unwilling to give up everything for the sake of Christ.

Julian was a successful executive in a global securities company. He always worked longer and harder than everyone around him, quickly climbing the corporate ladder. Behind his drive and energy was a need for recognition he never received as a child from his father. He came into a relationship with Christ through a friendship with David, one of his colleagues. Conversion was an ecstatic experience for Julian. He felt a peace that he had never had before; the guilt and shame he had carried about immoral choices he had made were lifted. He started attending a church and met with David weekly for a time of prayer.

Julian continued to advance in his career, which meant longer hours and increased travel. He felt elated about the affirmation he was receiving both publicly and in his paycheck. But it became more and more difficult for Julian to make the prayer time with David, and he stopped attending church since he was often out of town. When David asked Julian why he had stopped meeting with him, Julian rationalized by saying he didn't have time due to his increased responsibilities and there was nothing he could do about it. Years passed, and Julian became president of the company. He and David lost touch, until one day when they ran into each other at the airport. In the course of the conversation, David asked him where he was with his faith. Julian's response was, "Good question. I'm not sure I believe in God at this point."

Julian had been unwilling to surrender the esteem and accolades he garnered from his success. More passionate about following his career path than following God, he unwittingly lost out on walking a path to deeper intimacy with Him.

A. W. Tozer says that although humans are born rebels, we are sometimes unaware of it:

> [Man's] constant assertion of self, as far as he thinks of it at all, appears to him a perfectly normal thing. He is willing to share himself, sometimes even to sacrifice himself for a desired end, but never to dethrone himself. No matter how far down the scale of social acceptance he may slide, he is still in his own eyes a king on a throne, and no one, not even God, can take that throne from him.[7]

God is jealous for our hearts and will not take a second place to things this world considers valuable.

For still others, the invitation from God may seem too good to be true. Because of their lack of willingness to trust, they may hang onto life as it is and not relinquish control to God. The injustices and pain they have experienced may blind them to seeing that God actually desires good for their lives.

Karl grew up during the Depression, the youngest of four children in a deeply religious family. His father, an itinerant pastor, traveled to local communities teaching people about Jesus Christ. When Karl was in high school, his dad died suddenly and his mom died six months later. Between the loss of his parents and the daily scarcity of food, Karl had experienced a level of suffering by that time in his young life that many would not experience in a lifetime. To him, it seemed that God was cruel to allow his parents, who were so devoted, to go through so much pain. For Karl, this wasn't a God he wanted to follow. Throughout his life, he encountered many crossroads in which God was showing Karl His provision and care. Rather than trust that the good he was seeing was from God, Karl would credit it to his own talent, "luck," and hard work. By all accounts, Karl died without ever coming to know Christ. But it was clear, from those who knew him well, that God had been faithfully persistent in inviting Karl to realize His love for him. But God's love never overrides a person's choice to say no.

The condition of a person's heart is significant in this first stage and the life of a new believer. Jesus' parable of the sower powerfully illustrates this (see Matt. 13:1–23; Mark 4:1–20; Luke 8:4–15).

In this parable, Jesus tells the story of a farmer who sowed seed, which fell upon four types of soil. Some seed fell along the walking path where the birds ate it, so it didn't grow. The seed that fell in the rocks grew quickly in the shallow soil but then withered in the heat because it didn't have deep roots. The seed that fell among thorns was overtaken by weeds.

And finally, the seed sown in good soil grew and produced an abundant crop.

Jesus uses this story to explain "the nature of the kingdom in light of the nation's rejection" of Him.[8] Just as the leaders and others of that day either rejected or accepted the good news in the person of Jesus, so too, that message can be consumed by the world, wither when tried, choked by "thorns," or—as happens in Stage One—take root and grow when we answer Jesus' call to a saving faith.

While the condition of a person's heart—whether hardened or malleable in the hands of the Holy Spirit—can affect how the message of salvation is received, once we accept Christ, nurturing the "good soil" of our heart remains imperative. Mentorship, sound teaching, confession, and repentance are key at this stage if our new faith is to become deeply rooted and bear fruit.

TRANSFORMATION THROUGH SUFFERING

How we respond to pain will also indicate how we move through this stage. In this stage, it is not uncommon for someone to perceive suffering as a consequence for breaking God's laws and rebelling against Him. As mentioned in the previous chapter, our finite minds will never know the full reasons why God allows pain. But we do know that He always allows it for His loving purposes.

Carol was a college student when, during her summer break, she was involved in a near fatal car accident. When she woke up in the hospital, she talked through her shock with a friend, who was a believer, about nearly dying. With the jolt of the experience still fresh, she wondered aloud to her friend, "I guess God is trying to get my attention. I think I'd better listen." Carol then committed her life to following Christ. However, she also viewed what had happened as a consequence for not following God. Carol would learn in time that God allows trials in our life for a variety of purposes. Through pain, her false perceptions of God would be unveiled as would areas in which she didn't perceive God's love. Suffering would serve as a necessary conduit to teach Carol in this stage, onward.

Tim Keller summarizes the work of suffering:

> Some suffering is given in order to chastise and correct a
> person for wrongful patterns of life (as in the case of Jonah
> imperiled by the storm), some suffering is given not to correct
> past wrongs but to prevent future ones (as in the case of Joseph
> sold into slavery), and some suffering has no purpose other
> than to lead a person to love God more ardently for himself
> alone and so discover the ultimate peace and freedom.[9]

Carol's accident brought to light that fundamentally she was living her life on her own terms apart from God and His tender love for her . . . but God was not punishing her for her past unbelief.

Throughout our lives and faith journeys, we will keep returning to our first love and the joys of heaven that have been revealed. In this first stage of the soul, the life and love Christ invites us to enter into is to be conformed into His likeness in thought, word, and deed. It is to allow Him to live in us and through us so that the kingdom of God might be revealed. In addition, He calls us, on increasing levels, to the renewing of our hearts through His Word and presence. Our lives are Emmaus-road journeys; God walks along with us, making sense of our pain and bringing hope to our questions, as He did in the encounter recorded in the gospels of Luke and Mark. He continues to speak to us and direct us as He did His followers after His resurrection.

Every day, He invites us not only to receive His love but, by His Spirit, to live out the life of Christ to the world around us. He turns our "hearts of stone into hearts of flesh" (Ezek. 36:26). He asks to dwell in us in such a way that it is His hands that tenderly touch others who are in pain . . . His heart that shares in the heartache of others . . . His feet that bring words of encouragement to the hopeless. He is in the process of writing the most exquisite story through our lives as we say "yes" to His loving invitation. Day by day, we reflect more purely the image of Christ in our life so much that others might ask us how they too can have what we are radiating.

In the next chapter, we will look at how God deepens the faith of a new believer. We will see how God tenderly and wisely forms the believer's faith and vision to begin to live as Christ lived here on earth.

Summary of Key Characteristics of Stage One

- We are awakened into a relationship of our "first love" with God through Jesus Christ that leads us to salvation.
- We are invited by Jesus Christ to trust and follow Him in becoming like Him in our thoughts, words, and deeds.
- We are being restored by God to who He always intended us to be.
- We recognize the condition of the heart is critical in allowing God to shape and form us.
- We may be tempted to compromise our commitment to Christ by allowing the distractions of power, pleasure, esteem, and success to keep us from continuing to grow.
- We may perceive the suffering in our life as a consequence of leading a life apart from God.

Questions for Personal Reflection

1. How is my life different from before I chose to follow Christ?

_____

_____

2. In what ways did I live for my own self-rule and not God's?

_____

_____

3. How have I seen His love break through in my life?

_____

_____

4. What is the condition of the "soil" of my heart based on the parable of the sower and the seed?

_____

_____

AS YOU MOVE INTO THE NEXT CHAPTER: What knowledge or tools do you feel you lack for gaining a deeper understanding of what your life with Christ means?

STAGE TWO:
OBEDIENT LOVE

Learning the Ways of Godliness

For this very reason, make every effort to add to
your faith goodness; and to goodness, knowledge;
and to knowledge, self-control; and to self-control,
perseverance; and to perseverance, godliness;
and to godliness, mutual affection; and to mutual
affection, love. For if you possess these qualities in
increasing measure, they will keep you from being
ineffective and unproductive in your knowledge
of our Lord Jesus Christ.

2 PETER 1:5–8

At Harvard University, there is a class that has been offered that has exceeded all of the enrollment records in the history of the university. Each time this course is offered the enrollment exceeds eight hundred students. This class is entirely different from all others offered. It is known as a class on "happiness," or Positive Psychology 1504. If we can deduce anything from its popularity, it is that people are looking for happiness in record numbers, but it may be because we are "unhappier" than ever before and looking for love, peace, and hope.

David Myers, a professor of psychology at Hope College in Holland, Michigan, researched the pursuit of happiness, which he calls the American paradox:

> Maybe you, too, received the pass-along e-mail about the "paradox of our time": We have "bigger houses and smaller families, more conveniences but less time, steep profits and shallow relationships. We've learned how to make a living, but not a life; we've cleaned up the air, but polluted the soul.". . .
>
> Yet, paradoxically, we are a bit less likely to say we're "very happy." We are more often seriously depressed. And we are only now beginning to emerge from a serious social recession: doubled divorce, tripled teen suicide, quadrupled juvenile violence, quintupled prison population, and sextupled proportion of babies born to unmarried parents.[1]

As a college student in the '70s, I too was trying to find happiness and figure out the meaning of life. The 1970s were known for anti-war protests, the Watergate scandal, the women's rights movement, and Earth Day rallies. Back then, as today, students were searching for happiness, truth, love, hope, and peace.

This was the cultural backdrop as I entered my college years as a wide-eyed, idealistic explorer seeking to learn and experience as much as I could. My peer group ranged from the "brainiacs," those who were studying 24/7; the "frats," those who were partying Thursday through Sunday; and the "nerds," outcasts who never fit in anywhere and were agonizingly aware of it. I drifted through these groups as a spectator trying to figure out the meaning of life. By the end of my freshman year, I had almost flunked out, watched a gifted student fry his brains on drugs and another enter the fast track to alcoholism. I spiraled into an existential crisis, asking: What is the point of life? What really matters? Why does God allow suffering? Determined to find answers, I spent the summer of that year dedicated to a quest for truth and how God fit into the whole equation called "life."

How did Christ practically fit into "life"? While I had made a decision to follow Christ in middle school, I never learned how to practically live it out. I was familiar with the idea that there were nuns that prayed twenty-four hours a day and assumed that because of that, they knew something about devotion to God. Perhaps the answer to my question about how to live a life of devotion to God was becoming a nun. I decided to put a "fleece" before God. If a devoted Christian meant becoming a nun, then I would need to know by the second week of the semester so I could get my tuition refunded. I needed a sign.

I started the fall semester of my sophomore year with eyes alert to signs and miracles. I finally got my sign, but in a way I had never expected. Two days before classes started, I got a call from a student who had found my school ID, which had dropped out of my pocket. We arranged to meet. After producing my misplaced ID, he proceeded to tell me that he was a "born again" Christian and shared the gospel with me. Over the next two weeks, "born again" Christians seemed to be popping up on every corner. One day, I was stopped in the stairwell of my dorm by an odd-looking fellow with a button on his coat that read: "Wise men still seek Him." He gazed intensely into my eyes, and in a low, serious voice asked, "Do you know my Father?" I was stunned. I shrugged my shoulders and kept walking. A few days later, there was a knock on my door. The student standing there said that *God had sent her* (how do you not listen after an opening statement like that?) to talk with me and proceeded to share with me the message of Jesus Christ.

No need to start calling convents about admission; my answer was clear—God was inviting me back to my first love and to learn how to daily live my life with Jesus Christ. Alone in my dorm room one night, my head in my hands as I gazed at an open Bible, this searching wanderer found peace.

Providentially, I did not need to ask anyone how to be a Christian as I was surrounded by enthusiastic believers from two parachurch organizations—Campus Crusade (now called CRU) and InterVarsity Christian Fellowship—who directed me through the next steps. I started attending a class for new believers to understand the fundamentals of the faith, read my Bible daily, and got to know other believers at weekly gatherings. I learned about social justice issues, the role of spiritual gifts, and spiritual practices like fasting, discipleship, and evangelism. I was like a baby duck to water.

Looking back, I see how tenderly God had provided a rich foundation for me to build upon. I knew without a shadow of a doubt what I believed and why I believed it. I didn't realize it at the time, but I was moving into the Second Stage of faith, *Obedient Love and Learning the Ways of Godliness.*

CHARACTERISTICS OF STAGE TWO

The life of a new Christian is both exciting . . . and unnerving. People are generally full of questions: What do I do now? Should I attend church? Where should I go? What if I have doubts? How often should I pray and read the Bible?

The background of the believer before coming to Christ can greatly influence their present life with Christ. For those coming out of a lifestyle of addiction, there will be a need to separate themselves from triggers associated with their prior life. People who have come from other religions or a particular philosophy will need training in understanding the Bible and doctrine of the faith. As a new person in Christ, one's newfound values will affect friendships previously formed with nonbelievers. Relationships that were often marked by surface level conversation are now replaced with conversations with other believers that have a spiritual depth and meaning.

When we move from Stage One to Stage Two, our souls need to be formed by the biblical truths and the new ways of living our life with Christ. We need to know the essential information about the nature of God, the person of Jesus Christ, the work of the Holy Spirit, and the guidance of Scriptures, as well as what it means to balance right theology with healthy practices.

It is also critical at this stage that we live our life with other believers. In the context of these relationships, we learn how to practice the teachings of Jesus. Learning the depth and breadth of the truths of Scripture will also be paramount in order that our thoughts and values be formed into the way of Christ. We must study the Scriptures in such a way that they become part of our thinking and living. Lastly, spiritual practices like prayer, fasting, and times of solitude and silence will assist us in opening up a space in our souls for God to change us.

In this second stage of Obedient Love—Learning the Ways of Godliness, a new life in the kingdom is encapsulated in the Beatitudes (Matt. 5:1–12). Through these, Jesus invited His followers to a whole new way of seeing God, themselves, and life. He knew that it would be paramount for His followers to understand the fundamentals of what life in the kingdom of God entailed. The Beatitudes serves as a condensed guidebook for the new follower of Christ. It is the portion of Scripture that not only teaches the believer the heart of a follower of Jesus but living in the present reality of the kingdom of God. The Beatitudes, the eight blessings, are a picture of the heart and life of a disciple.

> Now when Jesus saw the crowds, he went up on a mountainside and sat down. His disciples came to him, and he began to teach them.
> He said:
>
> "Blessed are the poor in spirit,
>   for theirs is the kingdom of heaven.
> Blessed are those who mourn,
>   for they will be comforted.
> Blessed are the meek,
>   for they will inherit the earth.
> Blessed are those who hunger and thirst for righteousness,
>   for they will be filled.
> Blessed are the merciful,

for they will be shown mercy.
Blessed are the pure in heart,
for they will see God.
Blessed are the peacemakers,
for they will be called children of God.
Blessed are those who are persecuted because of righteousness,
for theirs is the kingdom of heaven.
Blessed are you when people insult you, persecute you and
falsely say all kinds of evil against you because of me. Rejoice
and be glad, because great is your reward in heaven, for in the
same way they persecuted the prophets who were before you.
(Matt. 5:1–12)

The Beatitudes guide the follower of Jesus in how to live in the kingdom of God but yet still live in the kingdom of this world. Jesus is offering a new way of living and turns the worldly idea of success and happiness on its head. The temptation is to read the Beatitudes as a list of behaviors that we must try to practice. We think we need to *be* poor, *act* mournful, *behave* as one who is meek, etc. The Beatitudes are not a list of requirements but rather a description of the kind of heart and soul that exemplifies a follower of Jesus Christ. Each Beatitude builds on the one before it[2] culminating in a full realization of what it means to be a radical follower of Christ fully formed in His image. Let's look at each of these attributes of a believer more closely.

"Blessed are the poor in spirit, for theirs is the kingdom of heaven" (Matt. 5:3). What a surprising way for Jesus to begin His teaching. What does Jesus mean by this? The term "blessed" is the Greek word *markarios*.[3] To be blessed is to live in the divinely appointed favored state with God.

The word "poor" in the Greek is *ptochoi*, which means "the very empty ones, those who are crouching."[4] Jesus is saying, blessed are the empty ones, those who are bent over with the weight of life's hardship and spiritually destitute. Yet, happy are they; they are the ones who will receive the kingdom of heaven. One commentator writes, "In some ways the Lord's declaration of 'blessed' is a pledge of divine reward for the inner spiritual character of the righteous; in other ways, it is His description of the spiritual attitude and state of people who are right with God."[5]

The higher we are within the systems of this world, the more influence and power we have, the more we are trapped and defined by those systems. The more wealth we have, the more we will do what we need to do to keep that wealth. Jesus is saying that those who have lost all semblance of worldly influence and power—the ones who can't afford to play the games of the world—"theirs is the kingdom of God."

This beatitude is the foundational truth by which everything else will follow. To follow Christ is to daily recognize the brokenness, sin, wounds, and pride that keep us from realizing our need for God. We need a Savior.

"Blessed are those who mourn, for they will be comforted" (Matt. 5:4). When we recognize the impact of our sin and its effects on us and on others, we will mourn.[6] We see our helplessness to make anything good out of our lives. We grieve over the damage our actions have caused others and ourselves as bearers of God's image. In Stage Two, we are keenly aware of our life prior to accepting Christ as our

Savior and the consequences of the choices we made apart from Christ.

"Blessed are the meek, for they will inherit the earth" (Matt. 5:5). Meekness is directly linked with a broken heart and mourning over sin. Meekness is a letting go of our right to be right. One writer defines meekness as "an active and deliberate acceptance of undesirable circumstances that are wisely seen by the individual as only part of a larger picture."[7] Everything we have is a gift from God. Therefore, there is nothing we "deserve." Freely we have received from God, not from our merits or striving, but because all is a gift (Matt. 10:8b). We then live our lives no longer needing to prove and defend ourselves to others; we see Christ as our defender and protector.

"Blessed are those who hunger and thirst for righteousness, for they will be filled" (Matt. 5:6). When we continue to live in poverty of soul, recognizing our need for God's mercy, God comforts us and develops in us a hunger for living the life He intended. Jesus is saying that, as we follow Him, we will hunger for the things of the kingdom in our own lives. He is the one who quenches our thirst: "Let anyone who is thirsty come to me and drink. Whoever believes in me, as Scripture has said, rivers of living water will flow from within them" (John 7:37–38).

"Blessed are the merciful, for they will be shown mercy" (Matt. 5:7). Mercy is derived from the Hebrew word *hesed*—the lovingkindness of God. It is because of God's lovingkindness, His mercy, that He has given us His Son. When we continue to hunger for God and become wholly devoted, we are able to realize on increasing levels what we have been redeemed from. Forgiveness and mercy go hand in hand. We will never truly understand mercy until we need it. Mercy is the very heart of God and Christ's excruciating death on the cross.

In this stage, we see how much we have been forgiven by God and can extend that easily to others. When others hurt and harm us, we are able to extend tenderness, kindness, and compassion.

"Blessed are the pure in heart, for they will see God" (Matt. 5:8). As we continue to grow in knowing Christ, our soul's one desire becomes to see Him more clearly in our daily lives. This Beatitude speaks to the singularity of one's vision. Jesus said that if the eye is pure, the whole body is full of light. What is a pure heart? A pure heart is one that is free of the masks of self-deception and duplicity. It is a heart that stands humbly before "the God who sees" (Gen. 16:13–14) and drops all pretense. The pure in heart only desire to fulfill the will of God in this world. In this stage, we allow Him to transform our thinking so we perceive the world through His eyes.

"Blessed are the peacemakers, for they will be called children of God.

"Blessed are those who are persecuted because of righteousness, for theirs is the kingdom of heaven."

"Blessed are you when people insult you, persecute you and falsely say all kinds of evil against you because of me. Rejoice and be glad, because great is your reward in

heaven, for in the same way they persecuted the prophets who were before you" (Matt. 5:9–12).

To be a son or daughter of God is to be like Christ. Sons and daughters of God are peacemakers, and peacemakers are reconcilers. Jesus came to reconcile women and men to God and to one another. Ephesians 2:14–15 states: "For he himself is our peace [*shalom*], who has made the two groups one and has destroyed the barrier, the dividing wall of hostility, by setting aside in his flesh the law with its commands and regulations."

This is the pinnacle of the Beatitudes and may very well be the most difficult to live out, not only for the new believer in Stage Two but even for those in deeper soul stages. While the other Beatitudes address the qualities of the follower of Christ, Jesus finishes by stating what will happen to His followers who are faithful. If we are genuinely peacemakers, then this will be the result. This is a radical promise. No rabbi ever called for his followers to die for his name or teaching. Like Jesus, peacemakers usually find themselves misunderstood and rejected and labeled with every possible moniker, but Jesus calls them the sons and daughters of God.

In summary, the Beatitudes, in the second stage, lay out for us the framework of what it means to live in the kingdom of God in our everyday lives while inviting us to the depth of what it means to be formed into Christlikeness. They are also a litmus test for mature believers to examine our hearts against Christ's description of what the heart of a disciple looks like.

On a daily level, we must continually recognize our helplessness to make anything good out of our lives without Christ. We cannot be sincerely loving people on our own merits. When we shout at our kids or say an unkind word about someone, we know that God continually extends to us His lovingkindness and mercy when we fail, calls us to repentance and from repentance to maturation.

Everything we have, all of who we are, is a gift from God, so we need not worry about how we will pay our bills or whether we get the job promotion. As we see His sufficiency in all things, we will find that we desire more time alone with Him and that nothing satisfies us more than knowing His love.

OBSTACLES TO GROWTH

In this second stage, where we are learning the ways of obedience, our hearts and lives are being shaped into the heart of God. However, a number of temptations can occur at this stage that can detour a person from appropriating and allowing God to form in us the qualities spelled out in the Beatitudes. Consequently, we will not continue to grow.

First, we may be tempted to avoid reflectively examining our lives and hearts before God on a daily basis. We can become so busy with "doing" the Christian life that we fail to practice the daily examination of our souls to see if we are actually "becoming" more like Christ. We can deceive ourselves with the notion that if we speak about the teachings of Jesus, study them, memorize them, and talk about them, then somehow we are actually *living* them. We can default to the misconception that our external behavior and beliefs are the sole measure of what is in our hearts. Although the "fruit" of our faith can be such a measure, we also need to be aware of our motivations.

Laura was a student in one of my classes. She was industrious and consistently received high grades. I was lecturing on Jesus' command that we must die to ourselves and remarked that many of us need to die to our religious pride, often displayed in "doing things for God." Laura found me after class and was clearly agitated. "Are you saying," she asked, "that the way I serve God is about pride?" While I wasn't directing my lecture toward her specifically, my comment prompted a troubling revelation for her. She had been working so hard for God she had never considered her motivations. She saw herself as faithful and serving God sacrificially but had not begun to exercise interior reflection before God.

As we have seen, Jesus is clear that the formation of the soul at this stage is to allow God to form and shape our inner hearts. The test for every believer is a constant recognition of our sin, pride, and pain. We must see a continual daily need for redemption and, at the same time, recognize the breadth and depth of the love of God.

The spiritual practice of confession then becomes a daily part of our lives. God is always bringing forth, on increasing levels, the fruit of the Holy Spirit. The fruit of the Spirit is realized as He brings His light to bear on the dark places and attitudes within our hearts. Caution is in order if we find it has been days since we have recognized a need to confess anything.

The daily practice of examining one's soul can be helpful in this regard. Taking time at the end of the day to review our attitudes, actions, and activities in the presence of Christ can help us to slow down and see where we have acted out of wrong motivations or our own self-serving pride.

A second obstacle is black and white thinking. Small children see the world as the "good guys" and the "bad guys." Some of us continue to carry that childlike thinking into our belief systems. Out of fear and a need to protect what we perceive as "right," we use our beliefs as a weapon to determine who is "in" the kingdom and who is "out," who is "bad" and who is "good." We then judge people according to our standards and, on behalf of God, assess the spiritual lives of others. This is the sin of the Pharisees that Jesus condemned. (See Luke 11:37–54.) This is in contrast to the believers in the church of Berea who had a positive and faith-filled attitude to God's world that was curious and open. (See Acts 17:11.)

To follow Jesus is to take seriously His admonition that we must take the "log" out of our own eye before we address the "speck" in someone else's eye (Matt. 7:5). If we don't see a need to confess anything, we must seriously question if we are following God or if we have put ourselves on the throne. If we fully attend to our own sin first, we will have little time or interest in judging the lives of others.

TRANSFORMATION THROUGH SUFFERING

In this stage of obedient love, the believer will tend to view suffering and trials through the lens of discipline of their

Heavenly Father. While from a finite perspective we will never fully know God's purposes, in this stage, the believer will tend to speak about their suffering as discipline and as an avenue by which God is growing them. God does use hardship as a gentle shepherd to guide us in the right path and to train us to listen to His voice above all the other voices.

The author of Hebrews speaks to this:

> And have you completely forgotten this word of encouragement that addresses you as a father addresses his son? It says,
>
>> "My son, do not make light of the Lord's discipline,
>>   and do not lose heart when he rebukes you,
>> because the Lord disciplines the one he loves,
>>   and he chastens everyone he accepts as his son."
>
> Endure hardship as discipline; God is treating you as his children. For what children are not disciplined by their father? If you are not disciplined—and everyone undergoes discipline—then you are not legitimate, not true sons and daughters at all. Moreover, we have all had human fathers who disciplined us and we respected them for it. How much more should we submit to the Father of spirits and live! They disciplined us for a little while as they thought best; but God disciplines us for our good, in order that we may share in his holiness. No discipline seems pleasant at the time, but painful. Later on, however, it produces a harvest of righteousness and peace for those who have been trained by it. (Heb. 12:5–11)

The believer is learning that God's love includes His divine "course correction" as they follow Him. Unlike earthly parents, God's discipline is never from anger or to punish. He is our perfect parent, guiding and growing us up in the ways of life in Him. As the passage in Hebrews indicates,

God's discipline is a token of our adoption as His children. God's purpose in discipline is to make us holy. God's holiness and His unique call of obedience will look different in each one of us. Arloa Sutter's response to God's call has left a legacy for many to follow.

In 1992, Sutter was serving in a church in Chicago, where the homeless would often come into the church office requesting money. Sutter felt it was more respectful to offer to pay them for work, so she would have them clean up the area around the church building. She explains, "It was more dignifying to give people a paycheck than a handout. I think it did a lot to sensitize people to the homeless and see them as real people who had something to offer to the community."[8]

In further response to the need, Sutter opened up a storefront to serve meals to the homeless as well as a shelter within the church. Word quickly spread among the poor, and the storefront became filled with hurting people telling stories that broke Sutter's heart. These most vulnerable ones also became her teachers.

In obedience to God's stirring in her heart, she determined to spend the rest of her life coming alongside the homeless and started Breakthrough Urban Ministries for the purpose of serving the needs of homeless adults, youth, and their families. As Sutter continued to grow in her obedience to Christ, her depth of understanding of Christ's love grew too.

She shares one of the experiences God used to teach her about the work He had called her to do:

I experienced my own epiphany of ministering to Jesus when Charles came to Breakthrough. He was obviously in great pain. He complained that his feet hurt. He was an elderly man who had difficulty reaching down to care for his feet. He had been walking all night to stay warm and was exhausted. I knelt down and gingerly removed his worn-out shoes from his feet and then his crusty socks. His feet were cracked and bleeding and gave off an obnoxious odor.[9]

Sutter filled a dishpan with soapy water and gently washed, dried, and rubbed lotion on Charles's feet.

Suddenly it was as if the whole present reality of what I was doing in the physical world gave way to the profound realization that Jesus had asked us to do this very thing—to wash one another's feet—and what I was doing for this lonely, old man, I was, in a sense, doing to Jesus himself. I felt such awe and joy and intimacy with Jesus at that moment.[10]

Through great sacrifice, Sutter has followed Christ, living among "the least of these" and bringing tangible resources and Christ's message of hope to them. Her obedience has been a model to many of the internal transformation of the heart that leads to eternal fruit in the kingdom of God.

In the next stage, we will look at God maturing the faith and soul of the believer and why many Christians remain in that stage for much of their journey.

Summary of Key Characteristics of Stage Two

- We learn the Bible's fundamental principles and practices of life with God and other believers.
- We learn to walk in obedience with Him and His ways.
- We find relationships with other believers guide us to greater understanding of what it means to live in the kingdom of God.
- We can become tempted to pride ourselves in our knowledge about God rather than becoming the people who are marked by the heart of God.
- We can also be tempted to serve and do acts of kindness for the recognition and approval of others rather than for Christ Himself.
- We may see suffering through the lens of God's discipline to mature us in becoming like Him.

Questions for Personal Reflection

1. Where do I need further training in growing in godliness?

_____

_____

2. How do I see my relationship with Christ changing me? Is it noticeable to those closest to me?

_____

_____

3. Do I serve for the approval of others or for God alone?

_____

_____

4. Is self-righteousness evident in any area of my life?

_____

_____

AS YOU MOVE INTO THE NEXT CHAPTER: Where do I experience suffering through which God is inviting me to a greater dying of my selfish tendencies?

Questions for Personal Reflection

1. Where do I need further training in growing in godliness?

_____

_____

2. How do I see my relationship with Christ changing me? Is it noticeable to those closest to me?

_____

_____

3. Do I serve for the approval of others or for God alone?

_____

_____

4. Is self-righteousness evident in any area of my life?

_____

_____

AS YOU MOVE INTO THE NEXT CHAPTER: Where do I experience suffering through which God is inviting me to a greater dying of my selfish tendencies?

STAGE THREE: PERSEVERING LOVE

Invitation to Intimacy

This life is not godliness, but growth in godliness;
not health, but healing; not being, but becoming;
not rest, but exercise. We are not now what we shall
be, but we are on the way; the process is not yet
finished, but it has begun; this is not the goal, but it
is a road; at present all does not gleam and glitter,
but everything is being purified.

MARTIN LUTHER

A Defense and Explanation of All Articles, AE 32:24

The journey up to this point has been fairly straightforward. We have encountered God's love, and we follow the guidebook of the Scriptures; we pray, we serve, we love. It all seems pretty clear. We have developed a certain "comfortableness" in our walk with God that seems to work. We want to please Him by doing what is right and following His commandments. Our faith, for the most part, is one of living from the outside in rather than the inside out. God is not wanting a "quid pro quo" relationship, wherein He does His part and we do ours, based on some unspoken working agreement. The life with Christ is not merely about correcting our bad habits but about meeting and satisfying our deepest longings; that is, for a deeply satisfying love and connection with God. Author Donald Miller described our relationship with Christ as more like a marriage than a formula.[1]

But the journey with Christ, like any journey, has unexpected sharp turns, rocky places, and detours on the path. Just when we think we are making progress, we encounter a bend in the road. Stage Three is that bend in the road. Things start happening in our life that we had not expected. We may lose our job or a child is diagnosed with a chronic illness or a close friend passes away. Or perhaps it is something far more elusive like a sense of spiritual boredom or apathy. Life with Christ no longer seems predictable.

That's because God loves us too much to allow us to stay in our places of comfortableness and control. He desires to help us gain an eternal perspective . . . to see things through His eyes. In Stage Three, God is inviting us to a deeper knowing of Him and a deeper knowing of ourselves.

Dieter Zander could never have predicted the bend in the road that God providentially ordained for him. Zander was a rare mix of extraordinary worship leader and tenderhearted shepherd. In the 1990s he was hired on at Willow Creek Community Church in Barrington, Illinois, to develop their Generation X "Axis" ministry. Thousands came to hear him lead worship and teach. John Ortberg, in his book, *Soul Keeping*, describes Zander:

> [Zander] led worship with so much vigor that at times he [literally] left blood on the keyboard from cracked fingernails. He led with such energy that we actually had to stop doing certain songs because people in the balconies jumped around too much and the facilities engineers were afraid the whole thing would come down—a kind of joy-driven variation of Samson and the Philistines.[2]

In time, Zander moved back to California to help pastors and ministry leaders think creatively about ministering to the upcoming generations. Then late one night, at the age of 47, he started trembling violently, suffering a massive stroke on the right side of his brain. He went into a coma and awoke six days later. The stroke left him with a crippled right hand and the inability to speak. He could no longer sing and lead worship. Pronouncing his own name came with great effort; words were trapped in his mind. His former eloquence was replaced with awkward pauses as he stumbled to find the right word.

Suddenly, the crowds, the performances, and the six-figure salary that made Zander, Zander, were gone. For a time, he lived alone in his friend's small shed in the backyard trying to make sense of what had happened. He writes:

> I was alone, and I realized my family is suffering, my job is never coming back, my ability to work and earn is gone, I can't lead, sing, teach, or pastor and I'm thinking "I'm done. I want to die." Suicide starts to run through my mind . . . Everything I thought was important and essential for my life is stripped

STAGES *of* THE SOUL

away, and I am left totally bare. And in that shack, God speaks
to me and says, "Dieter I love you." And I realize it's not my
leadership, or my singing or my performance that God loves.
Even when all that is gone God tells me—just as I am, all
alone with nothing—I am loved.[3]

Another time Zander says:

> My kingdom used to be a stage. A microphone. A piano, and
> an audience of thousands. My kingdom was a performance. A
> show. A sham. Then came the stroke. Now, five days a week,
> I arrive at Trader Joe's in the early dark, hours before the sun
> cracks the horizon. I push my mop up and down aisles, sweep
> my broom into corners to collect the debris from the day
> before. The store is quiet, empty. There is one audience in this
> kingdom. But that's ok, because I'm not performing. There is
> no Stage Dieter here.[4]

God was stripping away from Zander all the things that
were in the way of him entering into a deeper knowing of
God and knowing himself as a child of God. His relationship with Christ moved from a "working" relationship to
one marked by an intimate knowing. He explains: "God was
my boss. God is my friend now. God says, 'Dieter, you are
not going to work. Now, we play.'"[5]

CHARACTERISTICS OF STAGE THREE

Hidden blessings always lie within the trials we experience.
While we may not have a life-altering experience like Zander's, in this stage, God is inviting us to let go of all the ways
we define ourselves and the things our hearts are attached to

that keep us from drawing closer to Him. Fundamentally, we either live our lives trusting ourselves or trusting God.

In Stage Two, Obedient Love, we learn the basics of the Christian life, as if putting on an outer garment to cover ourselves. However, in Stage Three, Persevering Love— Invitation to Intimacy, God invites us to recognize the ways the "garment" of our faith may be covering the motivations of our hearts. We may behave like a follower of Christ, but our motivations and the inner workings of our hearts may still be driven by our personal agendas.

We can only come to know, on the deepest levels, that we are loved through moments of raw vulnerability and when we feel ourselves most exposed. Indeed, our transformation into Christlikeness is "a continuing process that unfolds one day at a time as we bring more and more of ourselves to God."[6]

It is one thing to be told you are loved; it is another thing to actually experience and allow that truth to settle into the intimate parts of your soul when instead your life feels out of control. Not until Zander was most vulnerable was he able to see the truth, in the deepest part of his soul, that he is loved unconditionally.

But we resist this. Everything in us wants others and God to see us at our best. We want to believe we really are good people with good motives; we don't want to be exposed as sinful and helpless. But this is the "false self," the self of our own making that still may linger even after we believe.

A recent personal experience served as a powerful—albeit embarrassing—metaphor for this:

I was flying from O'Hare International Airport in Chicago to a conference. On my way to the gate, I rushed into the women's restroom. After I washed my hands, I picked up my luggage and dashed toward what I thought was the exit. Instead, I smashed right into a floor-to-ceiling mirror. Still not aware that I had run into glass, but rather "someone," I quickly apologized. Finally realizing I had run into myself, I quickly glanced around to see if anyone had noticed. To my relief, I was the only one in the restroom!

Later, as I chuckled to myself about the mishap, I realized the incident serves as a powerful metaphor: God masterfully crafts life situations so that we run headlong into ourselves. In Stage Three, we become acutely aware that there is nothing between us and God to hide behind. As God's light shines upon us, we are invited to reflect upon the hidden motivations of our hearts and our own inaccurate roadmap to happiness. In this stage, God reveals the imposter, or "false self," in each one of us that still attempts to cover our wounds, fears, insecurities, and sins . . . a self we often present as our true self.

The false self relates to what the apostle Paul describes as the "flesh" in his letter to the Corinthians. Although by accepting Christ we have put off the "old man" or "old way," believers can still act, think, and walk as we did before we were saved. In contrast, the "true self" is who we are in Christ. In Stage Three, God's primary work is to strip away the trappings of the false self so that we can live our lives more freely in our true selves—followers in intimate union and identification with Him. How do we know what the false self looks like?

The false self is, for Christians, the "good" and "acceptable" self we want to present to others. But within that self is the imperfect, needy, shame-filled, and prone-to-feeling-like-a-failure person who God sees and calls to holiness and maturity. Thomas Merton said we clothe this false self by winding our experiences, pleasures, and glory around ourselves like bandages so we are "perceptible" to ourselves and the world.[7]

Everything in us would prefer to be loved for the person we want everyone to believe we are. In actuality, the false self is covering up the darkness in our hearts.

Clinical psychologist James Finley explains:

> There is something in me that puts on fig leaves of conceal-ment, kills my brother, builds towers of confusion, and brings cosmic chaos upon the earth. There is something in me that loves darkness rather than light, that rejects God and thereby rejects my own deepest reality as a human person made in the image and likeness of God.[8]

Every one of us runs from this reality. But God lovingly invites us to acknowledge the aspects of the "flesh" that seem to linger in Stage Three, sometimes for years and, sadly, sometimes for the rest of our lives. Do you recognize any of these tendencies in your own life?

- Self-conscious and prideful
- Striving for position and status
- Striving for happiness in what we have or do
- Striving for affirmation and esteem of others

- Striving for control
- Striving to establish safety and security
- Striving for an image of perfection

Jesus is unmistakably clear concerning the "self" when He says: "If anyone would come after me, let him deny himself" (Luke 9:23 ESV), and "Whoever would save his life will lose it, but whoever loses his life for my sake will save it." (Luke 9:24 ESV). Robert Mulholland, author and professor, explains, "Jesus is not talking about giving up candy for Lent. He is calling for the abandonment of our entire, pervasive, deeply entrenched matrix of self-referenced being" so we can enter into a life of loving union with God that manifests itself in Christlikeness.[9]

God not only will show us aspects of Himself in this stage in order to draw us into this sacred place of knowing and being known, He will create a "holy longing." This holy longing might come in the form of restlessness and questioning: Is there more to the spiritual life than all of our "religious" activity and "right" behaviors? No matter how hard we try, pray, read Scripture, practice spiritual disciplines, and even increase our ministry activity, real joy may still elude us. Life may seem stale and meaningless. The times of joy and peace we experienced in stages one and two, when we first encountered Christ and were eager to know Him better, feel like a lifetime ago.

Such was the situation for Keisha, a mother of two young children and part-time consultant. One night, she shared with her husband how she felt that her relationship with Christ seemed flat, meaningless, and dry. She felt distant from God and wondered what she was doing wrong. She anticipated her husband would say something like, "Well, spend more time reading your Bible," or "Perhaps you need to get more involved in church activities." His response was not what she expected: "Keisha, I think you are afraid to let God love you." His words shook her to her core. "It was as if Jesus was standing right in the room," she explained, "asking me to look up into His face and experience His love. It was almost too overwhelming to take it all in."

God was allowing a sense of spiritual dryness to show her He was so much more than her routine and daily practices. He wanted to show Himself as one who desires simply to be with her.

How does God bring us into a deeper love for Him? How does He move us from this stage and toward the next? In this stage we are awakened to the ways in which we are continuing to live under our own rule. In Jesus' parable of the prodigal son, the turning point for the wayward young man happens when he comes to his senses and determines: "I will set out and go back to my father and say to him: Father, I have sinned against heaven and against you" (Luke 15:18). While this is generally used as an illustration for conversion, our lifelong journey with Christ is a continual "conversion" and a coming to the end of ourselves in a multitude of ways. Without an experience of "magnificent defeat,"[10] the son would never have reached this defining moment. The grace of his father led him home, just as the grace of our Father leads us back to Him.

"In Christian spiritual transformation," writes David

Benner, "the self that embarks on the journey is not the self that arrives. The self that begins the spiritual journey is the self of our own creation, the self we thought ourselves to be. This is the self that dies on the journey. The self that arrives is the self that was loved into existence by Divine Love. This is the person we were destined from eternity to become—the I that is hidden in the 'I AM.'"[11] The apostle Paul reminds us

> Since, then, you have been raised with Christ, set your hearts on things above, where Christ is, seated at the right hand of God. Set your minds on things above, not on earthly things. For you died, and your life is now hidden with Christ in God. (Col. 3:1–3)

In the realm of Christian spiritual formation, attributes of the "true" self stand in contrast to those of the false self, mentioned previously:

- Authentic and vulnerable vs. Self-conscious and aware of image
- Humble and free vs. Striving for position and status
- Contentment in God's provision vs. Striving for happiness in what we have or do
- Love and union with God vs. Striving for affirmation and esteem of others
- Surrender vs. Striving for control
- Security in God's protection vs. Striving to establish safety and security

OBSTACLES TO GROWTH

What does it look like if we say "no" to God's invitations to a greater knowing of Him and ourselves in the third stage? The love of God always allows for our free choice . . . and, yet, Gregory of Nyssa, a fourth-century bishop, warned: "Sin happens whenever we refuse to keep growing."[12]

One reason for refusing the invitation is that we may want to *feel* better before *getting* better. We may want relief from our painful circumstances more than we actually want God to change us through the pain. We may want a resolution of our circumstances without doing the hard work of learning what God is teaching us in our suffering. Consequently, we deny there is a problem or blame our pain on someone else.

A leader of a large ministry known for his larger-than-life personality was asked how he deals with pain. A bit perplexed by the question, he replied, "I really don't have pain. In fact, I have never had a bad day in my life." Indeed, he may never have experienced a bad day, but others around him surely have.

We also may refuse to release the things our hearts have held onto so tightly. Instead of allowing God to meet us at our deepest need, we set up idols such as money, love, and power in those places where we have unhealed wounds. For instance, a person who idolizes money looks at the quality of their life through the lens of financial security. Someone who sets up love as an idol may be emotionally needy or may love "father or mother . . . son or daughter" (Matt. 10:37) more than God. A person who idolizes success and power will constantly jockey for position in any environment regardless of work or social settings.[13]

Idols in our life will eventually destroy us. In order to move into the next stage of transformation, we must take seriously God's commandment to have no other gods before Him (Ex. 20:3).

TRANSFORMATION THROUGH SUFFERING

For many of us in Stage Three, the tearing down of idols—including the idol of our "false self"—may require divinely orchestrated circumstances or other earthly trials we can't control or explain but that God works through. My husband, Ray, had lost his job as an executive in the retirement industry. He had been unemployed for six months with no viable prospects. Our children were young at the time, and our family had no income and no answers to prayers. Ray and I were scared. Back then, I would have described myself as a "good" Christian doing all the right things. In fact, I naively believed that I was "doing" the Christian life so well that God was glad I was on His team! Consequently, it was painful and distressing to me that God did not seem to be answering our prayers for a job.

One day, the thought came to mind, "What if my faith is a myth? What if everything I have believed about God and Christianity is just a nice tale that worked for a while but just doesn't work anymore?" I struggled all day with the rationale that if I had bought into a myth, I could choose to not believe that myth anymore. I even imagined what I would say to my friends: "Christianity just didn't hold the intellectual validity I thought it did."

Then, like the prodigal, my disruptive moment happened, and I "came to my senses." Suddenly, I was undone by the presence of God—not a quiet, tender presence, but the holy, powerful, and captivating presence of my Heavenly Father. At that moment, I sensed Him saying, "If I never bless you again, I AM." I was shaken to my knees and could not speak. My life was not my own. My motives and pride were exposed. My pharisaic heart was revealed. I realized that my prayers were fueled by the expectation that because I was doing the right things for God, then He would do His part *as I thought it should be*. God revealed Himself as Truth and Holiness. I was undone by the total otherness and majesty of who He is.

God was using our painful circumstances to reveal Himself and to purify my stubborn and willful heart. In the days and weeks that followed, my eyes were opened to His love and provision in ways I would not have seen had I continued hanging onto my own religious false self and how I thought God should provide. I would have gone down a path of self-righteousness to cover for my unaddressed fears and insecurities.

In this stage of persevering love—invitation to intimacy, we have seen how God uses suffering to beckon us into a deeper knowing of Him. He strips away all the things that inhibit us from drawing close to Him—our wrong thinking, misguided values, unhealthy attachments, and even our unbiblical assumptions about Him—and exhibits more of His presence. R. C. Sproul writes, "It is precisely the presence and help of Christ in times of suffering that makes it possible for us to stand up under pressure."[14]

Yolanda was a woman Brennan Manning describes as one who, by God's grace, was able to stand up under life's pressure as she faced her last days of a battle with leprosy. She was thirty-seven years old, a mother of two teenage children who were not allowed by their father to visit their mother. Before the leprosy had destroyed her body, Yolanda had been breathtakingly beautiful; now she was dying, her body disfigured by the horrible disease.

As Manning anointed her head with oil and prayed with her, the room was filled with a brilliant light. He gazed upon Yolanda's face and commented to her that she seemed happy. Manning explains what happened next:

> With her slight Mexican-American accent she said, "Oh, Father, I am so happy." I then asked her, "Will you tell me why you're so happy?" She said, "Yes, the Abba of Jesus just told me that He would take me home today." I vividly remember the hot tears that began rolling down my cheeks.[15]

Yolanda died six hours later. Manning later found out that Yolanda was illiterate and had never read the Bible, although the last words she spoke were full of joy in the Lord and reminiscent of those in the Song of Solomon. Yolanda encountered a road that humanly seemed impossible to travel and was met with the fully satisfying presence of God.

In the next stage, as we continue to die to all that is not of God, we will find our lives taking a trajectory of joy we never could have imagined.

oblivion, Muriel is the joy of my life. Daily I discern new manifestations of the kind of person she is, the wife I always loved. I also see fresh manifestations of God's love—the God I long to love more fully."[2] For thirteen years, McQuilkin faithfully cared for his wife until her death in 2003.

CHARACTERISTICS OF STAGE FOUR

McQuilkin exemplifies the love of those who God has matured in Stage Four—Sacrificial Love—Living the Kingdom Here and Now. God had prepared McQuilkin to care for Muriel through all the prior years of sacrifice, trials, and testing that had stripped him of his ego and claim to personal rights. When the time came that Muriel needed him most, McQuilkin gladly gave up his career and public recognition to care for his wife. Such is the love of those in Stage Four.

The core of Stage Four is reflected in Paul's prayer in Ephesians 3:16–19:

> I pray that out of his glorious riches he may strengthen you with power through his Spirit in your inner being, so that Christ may dwell in your hearts through faith. And I pray that you, being rooted and established in love, may have power, together with all the Lord's holy people, to grasp how wide and long and high and deep is the love of Christ, and to know this love that surpasses knowledge—that you may be filled to the measure of all the fullness of God.

In Stage Four, we possess a knowledge of the breadth and depth of God's immense love that is intellectual and personal, individual and corporate, and we experience Christ dwelling, or "taking up residence," in our heart.[3] We have moved on from Stage Three—Persevering Love, where we have been purged of our ego attachments of power, prestige, security, and esteem. God has exposed the hidden motivations of our hearts, and we are invited into a life of joy and delight that defies description—a life with Christ as the bridegroom with His bride. The veil has been dropped from our souls revealing a deep knowing.

When we gaze upon Him, we are swept up into the unfathomable beauty of His presence. A. W. Tozer reminds us that this was Jesus' posture as well: "And our Lord Himself looked always at God. 'Looking up to heaven, he blessed, and brake, and gave the bread to his disciples' (Matt. 14:19). Indeed Jesus taught that He wrought His works by always keeping His inward eyes upon His Father. His power lay in His continuous look at God" (John 5:19–21).[4]

In Stage Four, our eyes are opened to the reality that "'in him we live and move and have our being'" (Acts 17:28). In some Christian traditions, this stage is called the Illuminative stage where our eyes are opened to see the magnificence of God. Thomas Merton explains, "We awaken not only to the realization of the immensity and majesty of God 'out there' as King and Ruler of the universe (which he is) but also to a more intimate and more wonderful perception of him as directly and personally present in our own being."[5]

And yet, in realizing the glory of His presence, we are aware more than ever of the darkness that remains within us. We recognize that we cannot accomplish good via our own efforts. Just as the moon can only reflect the light of the sun, so we can only reflect God's light, as the psalmist expresses: "In your light we see light" (Ps. 36:9). As the light of Christ more clearly shines on us, we see, with a high degree of acuity, the depravity of hearts apart from Christ.

François Fénelon, the sixteenth century theologian and writer, describes an experience of the type common in Stage Four:

> As that light increases, we see ourselves to be worse than we thought. We are amazed at our former blindness as we see issuing forth from the depths of our heart a whole swarm of shameful feelings, like filthy reptiles crawling from a hidden cave. We never could have believed that we had harboured such things, and we stand aghast as we watch them gradually appear. But we must neither be amazed nor disheartened. We are not worse than we were; on the contrary, we are better. But while our faults diminish, the light by which we see them waxes brighter, and we are filled with horror. Bear in mind, for your comfort, that we only perceive our malady when the cure begins. So long as there is no sign of cure, we are unconscious of the depth of our disease; we are in a state of blind presumption and hardness, the prey of self-delusion.[6]

Such sober awareness of what resides in our souls leads us to relying on the mercy of God to keep us from our own proclivities.

We see the apostle Peter—having betrayed Christ and having been "sifted like wheat" in his own Stage Three—initiated into Stage Four when Jesus re-commissions Peter by the Sea of Galilee to love and care for His flock. In the book of Acts, Peter, empowered by the Spirit, proclaims the gospel without hesitation and invites people to repentance.

Like Peter, the believer, too, is enabled and empowered by the Holy Spirit, and His work in the Christian is evident to others. We gladly and readily serve and love God's people; we are not concerned about what we receive in return because we daily rely on God's nurturance and are satisfied with how tenderly and intimately He loves us. We experience an increased capacity to extend grace and to do good and to love unconditionally. We are less judgmental and more accepting of others and desire to show compassion and mercy.[7]

Our lives begin to embody the Sermon on the Mount. We seek to love our enemies, forgive rather than condemn, and are willing to go the second mile with others. People see us as radiating God's light in the world. We have become so illumined by the truth of Christ that we embody His presence in the world.

Those in this sacrificial love stage, because of all that God has stripped away, have realized a certain degree of healthy unsettledness with this world. The attachments of this world no longer intrigue us. We are not troubled by the criticism of others. We see whatever is placed in our life as a conduit through which we can serve God and His kingdom.

The British journalist, Malcolm Muggeridge, said that ever since he could remember, he had a sense of being a stranger in this world. He writes, "The only ultimate disaster that can befall us, I have come to realise, is to feel ourselves to be at home here on earth. As long as we are aliens we cannot forget our true homeland."[8] The earthly longings for success, power, and security are but faint memories now. We have found Christ's promise to be true, that He is the "bread of life" and only He can provide the sustenance we need.

In Stage Three, our prayers may resemble more of a monologue about what we have and what we don't have than a dialogue with God. But in Stage Four, prayer has moved from listing our needs and requests to coming fully into God's presence. It has become more effortless and marked by a gentle knowing; it is the posture of John, the beloved apostle, leaning against Jesus as He talks with the disciples. (See John 13:23–25.) As a couple in love can comfortably sit in each other's arms without words, so we can be silent and "recline" with God in His presence, absorbing His truth, beauty, goodness, and love. As we dwell in this place, others may be drawn into the gentle and peaceful demeanor born from this place of prayer. This posture may appear—to nonbelievers and even Christians who have not reached this stage—as very "other."

In fact, those in Stage Four may be perceived to be "religious fanatics" because of the extremes (at least by the world's standards) to which their devotion to God may take them.

Maggie Gobran, a successful business executive and college professor, grew up in a wealthy family in Cairo, Egypt. During religious holidays, she often accompanied her Aunt Teda to the "garbage city" in Cairo to minister to the people and children living in squalor there. After her Aunt Teda passed away, Gobran continued the traditional visits. On one such visit, she noticed some movement in one of the mounds of garbage and uncovered a tiny child rummaging through the garbage for food. Gobran picked up the little girl and held her on her lap. For days afterward, she was haunted by the encounter, and she sensed God beckoning her to enter into a life of sacrifice for Him. Because she had allowed God to mature her in the faith, by that point she could do no other but accept His invitation to devote her life to caring for the children. She traded her designer clothes for a simple white cotton skirt and t-shirt spending her days bringing food to the starving children in garbage city.

Her friends and acquaintances ridiculed and criticized her, telling her she was crazy. They couldn't understand why she would want to be associated with people in the slums. Their judgment didn't detract Gobran; she had experienced God's goodness in her own life and felt that to love these vulnerable children was to love Christ Himself.[9] Gobran, today affectionately known as Mama Maggie, once said, "When I listen to a poor child, I'm listening to God's heart beating for all humanity."[10]

When my husband, Ray, and I met Mama Maggie and visited her ministry in the slums, we were unprepared for what we experienced. Donkeys pulled dilapidated carts overflowing with garbage down muddy streets, and mounds of recycled garbage made up the landscape. But at one of the pre-schools Maggie started, we saw children, who would normally be picking through garbage to help their families earn a few dollars, sitting at desks instead. Now surrounded by the love of Christ through the tireless energy and devotion of the school staff, the children were all smiles, their eyes bright with hope.

Mama Maggie's organization, Stephen's Children, has

reached more than 33,000 children caught in the snare of poverty.[11] Because of one woman's faithful obedience, many lives have been changed. Considered the Mother Teresa of Egypt, her service is Isaiah 58:10 lived out:

> . . . if you spend yourselves in behalf of the hungry
>   and satisfy the needs of the oppressed,
> then your light will rise in the darkness,
>   and your night will become like the noonday.

OBSTACLES TO GROWTH

At any soul stage, the sin of pride can be a major obstacle to growth; however, pride in Stage Four is far more insidious than in other stages. Those through whom the Holy Spirit has worked to the benefit of others and to whom God has revealed Himself can fall prey to seeing themselves as having advanced further in the kingdom than others. As such, we may deceive ourselves that we are set apart by God and therefore "special" and are above having to deal with the mundane issues of life. We may be tempted to a low grade dissatisfaction with our life that may be masking an unwillingness to suffer. We may deceive ourselves into thinking we actually embody the very principles we teach but lose track of our need for continued growth into holiness.[12]

A litmus test for the Stage Four soul is whether or not we are growing in humility—a self-forgetfulness as well as an awareness of our nothingness in light of a holy God. It may become necessary to step away from our work and daily lives in order to be reminded of who we are in Christ alone. This may involve an extended time of reflection and quiet prayer so we are able to hear the loving voice of God.

Another obstacle may occur in this stage—that of spiritual weariness. While weariness, like pride, can occur at any stage, it particularly raises its ugly head in Stage Four as a loss of drive and passion for service and even for our spiritual life when no tangible outcomes are evident. We may lose interest in spiritual practices, and the joy of doing God's work may become lost in daily tedium.[13]

But God can use even this to bring our soul to the next stage of transformation. Friedrich Nietzsche describes this journey well: "The essential thing 'in heaven and in earth' is, apparently . . . that there should be long OBEDIENCE in the same direction, there thereby results, and has always resulted in the long run, something which has made life worth living."[14] The call of this stage for the believer is the "long obedience": to continue to follow, to serve, and to sacrifice for Christ and the kingdom of God. Perseverance is imperative if the believer is to be faithful in service until the end and to hear the welcome words of our Father, "Well done, good and faithful servant" (Matt 25:23).

TRANSFORMATION THROUGH SUFFERING

Jesus had promised His followers that they would suffer for His name as He had suffered (John 15:20). Suffering, at this stage, while it doesn't exclude lessons from other stages, is primarily used by God to reveal His power and glory. We see this when Peter and John are arrested by the Sadducees for healing a cripple (Acts 4:3–22, 5:17–42), questioned by the Sanhedrin, and flogged (5:40). We see Stephen, "perform[ing] great wonders and signs among the people" (Acts 6:8b), brought before the Sanhedrin, boldly proclaiming the redemption of Christ and consequently being stoned.

Suffering can be caused by others—even fellow Christians—who may observe, and then envy, the spiritual power to which a person in this stage is used by God. Envy is a diabolical sin of the soul that feels it deserves what others have and, at its worst, can tempt a person to want to destroy another. An associate pastor envious of the "success" and spiritual flourishing of the senior pastor who is living in stage four may feel he deserves the recognition and position. He may incite others to find fault with the senior pastor and cause division. Consequently, the senior pastor will experience suffering, but so will the entire body.

Suffering in this stage can also be caused by long-lasting events that test our ability to persevere. Author Selwyn Hughes epitomizes the heart and attitude of the suffering believer in Stage Four: "I know from experience that whatever character has been built up in me, whatever of Christ's love and compassion flows through my life, has largely come about through suffering."[15]

In the space of two decades, Hughes lost his wife to cancer, his father to a heart attack, and his two sons within ten months of each other to liver disease and a massive heart attack. Hughes himself was later diagnosed with prostate cancer that spread into his bones. But that was not the end of his suffering . . . or of his spiritual growth. He continues:

In the last year I was diagnosed with "maturity onset diabetes" and a few months ago came close to losing the sight in my right eye through a detached retina. It will not be all that long now before some wise, white coated young doctor will look me over and put me in the NTBR (Not To Be Resuscitated). But through the emotional and physical suffering I have experienced, I have come to sense a new note in my ministry, a deeper compassion for those in need, and an increasing awareness that I am, as Scripture puts it, being made "perfect through suffering" (Hebrews 2:10, NIV).[16]

Hughes evidenced the growth toward holiness that occurs in our lives when we submit to the lessons God has for us.

We began this chapter with the story of Robertson McQuilkin and how he wisely lived out the characteristics of this stage. In his wife's last years, McQuilkin discovered that the demands on his time and energy became avenues by which he learned to love Muriel more. More astonishing was what God showed McQuilkin about Himself. McQuilkin explains:

No one ever needed me like Muriel, and no one ever responded to my efforts so totally as she. It's the nearest thing I've experienced on a human plane to what my relationship with God was designed to be: God's unfailing love poured out in constant care of helpless me . . . Surely he planned that relationship to draw from me the kind of love and gratitude Muriel had for her man. Her insatiable—even desperate— longing to be with me, her quiet confidence in my ability and desire to care for her, a mirror reflection of what my love for God should be.[17]

In this stage of sacrificial love lies the paradox that, as St. Francis prayed, in pardoning we are pardoned, in dying we are born to eternal life.[18] In allowing Christ to love through us and change us through suffering, we encounter His love in those we are called to compassionately care for.

But this is not the end of the ever-deepening spiral of knowing and loving Christ more. In the next chapter, we will see that the culmination of a life surrendered to Christ brings us to the fifth and final soul stage: intimate love.

Summary of Key Characteristics in Stage Four

- We are significantly freer from the bondage of our selfish sinful tendencies.
- We are fully satisfied with God above everything else and understand the depth of His love for us and the world around us.
- We are invited by God to a higher level of sacrifice, and, by His grace, we gladly show others His love by modeling the compassion, grace, and mercy of Christ.
- We are acutely aware of the condition of our own souls and the need for God's continual sanctification.
- We may be tempted to spiritual pride in falsely believing we are farther along than others.
- We may suffer as a result of others committing sin against us. God may also use suffering to help us develop perseverance.

Questions for Personal Reflection

1. Where do you see God's love most evident?

_____

_____

2. In this deeper love relationship with Him, in what ways do you see Him calling you to serve sacrificially? What is your attitude toward it?

_____

_____

3. How is God inviting you to a deeper understanding of your own sinfulness and need for confession?

_____

_____

4. In what ways are you tempted toward spiritual pride?

_____

_____

5. How do you fight the temptation of "growing weary in well doing"?

_____

_____

AS YOU MOVE INTO THE NEXT CHAPTER: What are the aspects of yourself and areas of your life that you still need to surrender in order to fully live and abide in the love of Christ?

STAGE FIVE:
INTIMATE LOVE

Being Light and Love for the World

Other great men may alter the material aspect of life
for millions, for generations, but the saints make us for
eternity. By emptying themselves, by getting rid of self
altogether, they become the channels of God's creative
power and by him, through them, we are made.

ELIZABETH GOUDGE

My God and My All: The Life of Saint Francis of Assisi

One of my favorite memories was when our children were small and used to cuddle up beside me for story time with one of my favorite children's books, *The Giving Tree* by Shel Silverstein. Though written for children, the story has a lasting message for all ages.

Every day a little boy would come to the tree to eat her apples, climb her trunk, and swing from her branches . . . and the tree would be happy. But as the boy grew older, he spent less time with the tree and only came back when he wanted something. To make him happy at each stage of his life, the tree gladly gave parts of herself: apples for him to sell and branches to build a house for his family and finally her trunk so he could build a boat to relieve him of his mid-life boredom.

In the final pages, the boy, now a frail old man, returns to the tree who now is just an old stump. The tree feels sad that she cannot provide shade, nor apples, nor materials to build for him. The old man is unfazed. He simply wants a place to sit. The tree responds that an old stump is good for that.[1]

The Giving Tree is a simple, yet poignant picture of the heart of God in Christ. Each day throughout His three-year ministry, Jesus healed, forgave, encouraged, loved, and taught—of a kingdom of human flourishing, wholeness, and delight. Christ showed us the unfathomable depths of His love through His willing submission to brutal torture and death. The cross, His "giving tree," became the most significant act of love to have ever existed. This is what Christ has modeled for us, and through the life of the Holy Spirit, we are also invited to bring the kingdom here on earth.

CHARACTERISTICS OF STAGE FIVE

Like the giving tree, we too realize the fulfillment of God's love in us and through us. Intimate Love—Being Light and Love for the World is the final stage for those who have persevered and faithfully followed Christ. For many Christians, this destination of transformation remains forever on the horizon. In the earlier stages of their faith journey, they decline God's invitations or become sidetracked by their own stubborn willfulness. But for those who want nothing less than to be "filled to the measure of all the fullness of God" (Eph. 3:19), this chapter will hopefully provide inspiration as well as a glimpse of the breathtaking landscape ahead.

In Stage Five, we reach a place of deep union with Christ. The believer in this stage has an unceasing awareness of God's intimate and loving presence, which has become so formed in the believer that the mind and will are perfectly attuned to carry out His loving purposes. We follow Jesus' model for living a life in union with the Father so that we can do only what we see our Father doing, because whatever the Father does we also do (see John 5:19).

Our surrender to God that began in earlier stages is now fully apprehended in Stage Five. The wounds and temptations that would have derailed us in the past hold no sway over us now. We realize, looking back on our journey, that all the losses, unexpected twists and turns in the road, and external and internal battles were necessary for drawing our souls to this deepest stage of knowledge and love.

C. S. Lewis understood the concept of this final union:

> The command *Be ye perfect* is not idealistic gas. . . . if we choose—He will make the feeblest and filthiest of us into a god or goddess, a dazzling, radiant, immortal creature, pulsating all through with such energy and joy and wisdom and love as we cannot now imagine, a bright stainless mirror which reflects back to God perfectly (though, of course, on a smaller scale) His own boundless power and delight and goodness.[2]

In a sense, our lives are transparent and reflect the eternal reality of Christ and all of who He is. As Jesus prayed in

John 17, so in this stage now, the believer's greatest desire is that God would be glorified . . . and that, like Jesus, we will be able to say: "I have brought you glory on earth by finishing the work you gave me to do (v. 4)."

God so enraptures the soul that we are oblivious to the drive for success, esteem, and security. Thus, we no longer have need for recognition from others and are completely content and surrendered. Even sin no longer has the same power over us, for God has so transformed the soul, we are no longer tempted to fall into any intentional sin.[3] Whatever circumstances we may find ourselves in, we see God's eyes upon it and His hands at work and consider it the greatest happiness to serve Him.

Such a posture of the heart and mind is summed up in the words Mother Teresa wrote: "The fruit of silence is prayer; the fruit of prayer is faith; the fruit of faith is love; the fruit of love is service; the fruit of service is peace."[4]

The culmination of formation that occurs at this stage has been described by Bruce Demarest, author and professor at Denver Seminary: "United with the Savior, disciples think with the mind of Christ, form intentions consistent with the will of Christ, feel with the emotions of and conduct themselves following the example of Christ."[5]

Another person who stands as an example of a believer who embodied this union and identification with Christ is Dallas Willard, a professor of philosophy and a modern day reformer of the church. His writing on spiritual formation skillfully and brilliantly exhorted the reader to consider the teachings of Jesus and the reality of the kingdom of God in its fullness here and now. He, following the example of Jesus, was able to tenderly and insightfully bring God's truth to the scholar as well as the unschooled worker. Authentically gracious, gentle, humble, and kind, Willard also lived out what he taught. He allowed himself to be so formed by God that he became God's light and love to whomever he met. People often commented how motivated they were to more passionately follow Jesus as a result of knowing Willard.[6] Dallas Willard passed into eternity in 2013, but for him, that passage was only the joyful completion of the journey he had been living so fully this side of heaven.

Aaron Preston, one of Willard's PhD students, sums up his teacher's life this way: "Two lines come to mind whenever I think of him. The first is from John's Gospel: 'No one ever spoke the way this man does' (John 7:46). The second is Plato's description of Socrates from the closing line of the Phaedo: 'The best, the wisest, and most righteous of all the men whom I have ever known.'"[7]

Believers in this stage have a love that goes beyond boundary lines and embraces the entire world. We see this in people like Billy Graham, one of the few people in history loved by people across the world because he was able to cross racial, political, and social divisions and present the message and person of Jesus Christ. Graham's personal pastor, who met with him weekly for more than fifteen years, describes Graham's prayer requests: "He would ask *me* to pray that God the Spirit would fill him to the extent that he would be totally hidden behind the cross and people would only see Jesus," and "His entire life was in pursuit that he would decrease so that Christ would increase."[8] Graham's attitude echoed the apostle Paul's words:

> Indeed, I count everything as loss because of the surpassing worth of knowing Christ Jesus my Lord. For his sake I have suffered the loss of all things and count them as rubbish, in order that I may gain Christ and be found in him, not having a righteousness of my own that comes from the law, but that which comes through faith in Christ, the righteousness from God that depends on faith—that I may know him and the power of his resurrection, and may share his sufferings, becoming like him in his death, that by any means possible I may attain the resurrection from the dead. (Phil. 3:8–11 ESV)

OBSTACLES TO GROWTH

As long as we are in this body of flesh, we will have temptations. At this stage, we have been "made perfect" through suffering but are still vulnerable to temptation. We may feel the battle of loneliness and discouragement when we find there are few people who understand the depth of peace and surrender we experience with God.

In addition, we may be criticized for our choices, which likely seem foreign to those who live by worldly standards. For instance, we may feel called to live among the poor and be criticized by our friends for not being a good steward of our resources.

In fact, we may face this stage seemingly alone, except for the companionship and assurance of the Holy Spirit, who supernaturally guides, strengthens, and sustains us on the last leg of the journey, no matter how impossible the terrain.

Like the apostle Paul, no matter the depth of the loneliness and hardship, we desire nothing more than to one day say, "I have fought the good fight, I have finished the race, I have kept the faith" (2 Tim. 4:7).

TRANSFORMATION THROUGH
SUFFERING—SHARING IN CHRIST'S SUFFERING

Sharing in Christ's suffering cannot be defined as the general pain and struggles of life. In Stage Five, sharing in Christ's suffering is sharing in Christ's mission of the redemption of humankind. Gordon Fee notes:

> Thus Christ's sufferings do not refer to "sufferings in general," but to those sufferings that culminated in his death, all of which was for the sake of others. Likewise, it is not just any kind of present suffering to which Paul refers . . . but to those which in particular express participation in *Christ's* sufferings; and the aim, as well as the character, of such suffering is to "become like him in his death," which almost certainly means suffering that is in some way on behalf of the gospel, thus for the sake of others, since no other suffering is in conformity to his.[9]

More specifically, in his letter to the Corinthians, Paul describes this in the trials he was experiencing as a result of proclaiming the good news of Christ:

> We always carry around in our body the death of Jesus, so that the life of Jesus may also be revealed in our body. For we who are alive are always being given over to death for Jesus' sake, so that his life may also be revealed in our mortal body. So then, death is at work in us, but life is at work in you" (2 Cor. 4:10–12).

As a result of bringing and being the light of Christ in a dark world, the believer in this stage experiences hardships such as false accusations, persecution, unjust suffering, and, for some, even martyrdom and death.

Today, millions of believers face the most extreme forms of persecution—from forced conversions and execution of believers in Iraq by ISIL and other extremists[10] to the government-led demolitions of churches and crosses in Zhejiang province, China.[11]

A. W. Tozer, in his book *The Root of the Righteous*, addresses human suffering and God's presence in it—whether it be the "howl of protest from the newborn" or the martyrdom of the servant. He writes:

> It is not possible that the afflicted saint should feel a stab of pain to which Christ is a stranger. Our Lord not only suffered once on earth, He suffers now along with His people. "Behold," cried the old saint as he watched a youthful martyr die. "Behold how our Lord suffers in the body of His handmaid."[12]

Yet, believers in Stage Five no longer fear death; they see it merely as a door to the ultimate reality. Heaven, for them, is the everlasting fullness of life with Christ and but also a continuation of becoming the people God always intended them to be.

"Every age, happily, has its heroes," writes May Quinlan. "Some die for country; others for a cause; some have sacrificed themselves for the many, others for an individual friend or stranger; but the sacrifice of Joseph Damien de Veuster was not as these. For though he died that others might live, his object was not so much to preserve the life of the body as to ensure the salvation of the soul."[13]

Jozef de Veuster, later called Father Damien or Damien the Leper, was born in Belgium on January 3, 1840. As a young man, he felt called to ministry. After ordination, he moved to Hawaii and served nine years as a missionary on the main island, from 1868–1873. During that time, leprosy (Hansen's disease) had reached epidemic proportions on the island. Since, at the time, there was no known cure, contracting the disease meant a lifetime of disfigurement, slow bodily decay, and certain death. Government officials were dispatched to round up anyone with symptoms of the disease for fear of contamination. People were violently separated from their families, and forced onto a cargo ship headed to a government-established leper colony on the small island of Molokai, where they were left to fend for themselves.

Death and despair marked the lives of those abandoned on the island—a place of lawlessness, sexual immorality, brawling, drunkenness, and robbery. No one cared for anyone else. When someone died, the body was thrown into a shallow grave.

The bishop of the churches in Hawaii was moved by the plight of the people and asked for priests to serve on Molokai. Damien was the first to volunteer. On May 10, 1873, he arrived and the bishop introduced Damien to the approximately 816 lepers as "one who will be a father to you, and who loves you so much that he does not hesitate to become one of you; to live and die with you."[14]

Wherever Damien looked, he saw disfigured faces and

dying bodies that exuded the foul odor of decay. He determined to love and care for them as Christ would. Six months after his arrival at the island he wrote his brother of his desire to be in solidarity with the lepers. He went on to explain, "That is why, in preaching, I say 'we lepers'; not, 'my brethren.'"[15]

Slowly, he gained the love and respect of the lepers by ministering to the sick, washing their bodies, bandaging their wounds, and doing everything he could to make them comfortable. Damien helped them build cottages to replace the grass huts they had originally constructed themselves. He taught them to raise farm animals and crops, giving them the ability to feed themselves. He built a home for the lepers' children, to provide safe and loving care. He encouraged their love of music, and they returned to singing together.

Damien was determined to restore their dignity and, as much as possible, help them return to a life of meaning and purpose. He spent countless hours telling the lepers, who once saw themselves as already dead, that God cared for them and that they were not alone in their suffering, successfully dispelling the myth that leprosy was God's punishment on unworthy sinners.

Eleven years later, in place of the miserable huts of the colony's beginnings, stood two villages of white houses, surrounded by flower gardens and cultivated fields. Edward Clifford, who visited Molokai, testifies to the transformation that occurred on the island: "The faces one sees are nearly always happy faces. One sees the people sitting, chatting at their cottage doors, or galloping on their little ponies between the two villages; and one always receives the ready greeting and the readier smile."[16]

Damien won the people's hearts through his sacrifice and love, and they won his heart. After sixteen years of living together with the lepers, Damien became a victim of leprosy as well and died among his beloved flock.

What gave Damien the courage to persevere in such harsh and lonely conditions? He was simply living and abiding in the presence of Christ, following in the footsteps of the One who had gone before Him, the One who stretched out His hand to the leper and healed him (see Mark 1:40-45). Jesus not only healed the leper, He also entered into the leper's world of despair, isolation, pain, and shame. So too Damien entered into that same darkness and touched the people of Molokai with Christ's compassion. He transformed the island from a place of horror, despair, and moral debauchery into one of faith, hope, and peace. Damien was one of the beloved saints who "did not love their lives so much as to shrink from death" (Rev. 12:11).

Few people allow themselves to grow to this final stage of faith. But the invitation is there for all of us to take up our cross and passionately follow Christ wherever He leads. In doing so, we allow Him, through suffering and trials, to shape us into His image—children of the living God, given power and authority to one day reign with Him.

THE END OF OUR JOURNEY TOGETHER

We have journeyed together throughout this book examining the five Stages of the Soul. We began with Stage One of being called into a saving faith with Christ. We then were invited by God to learn the ways of godliness and growing in obedient love (Stage Two). In Stage Three, God invited us to a love relationship that was marked by greater intimacy with God. The idols of the heart were brought to the surface, and we were being purified by Him. In Stage Four, God invited us to sacrificial love in order to usher in His kingdom here on earth. As we continue to allow Him to purify us, we are invited into an intimate union with Christ to become light and love to the world (Stage Five).

Knowing the terrain of the soul helps us to stay focused on our singular goal—to love God with all our heart, mind, and *soul* so that the kingdom of God will go forward.

No matter the stage we are in, we must continue to abide moment by moment in Him, keeping our gaze fixed upon His face and allowing Him to transform us. The apostle John reminds us that ". . . we are children of God, and what we will be has not yet been made known. But we know that when Christ appears, we shall be like him, for we shall see him as he is" (1 John 3:2). Indeed, we will finally behold Him, but we will never reach the end of knowing the fullness of the One who is "the Alpha and the Omega, the First and the Last, the Beginning and the End" (Rev. 22:13).

Summary of Key Characteristics in Stage Five

- We have a high degree of identification with Christ and a willingness to lay down our lives.
- We have become, by God's grace, perfect through suffering.
- We experience a deep union with Christ and want nothing more than to dwell with Him.
- We are seen by others as embodying God's light and love.
- We share in the sufferings of Christ that the gospel may go forward.
- We no longer fear death but rather see it as the full realization of seeing Christ face to face.

Questions for Personal Reflection

1. When you look back over your life, how have you seen God pursue you into a deeper awareness of His love?

_____

_____

2. In what way has suffering matured you to understand more of who you are in Him as well as the fullness of who He is?

_____

_____

3. In what ways has eternity become more real for you on a daily basis?

_____

_____

4. How do you find God meeting you when you encounter times of loneliness?

_____

_____

AS YOU LOOK TO ETERNITY: What legacy of faith do you hope to leave as a marker for the journeys of others?

BEFORE WE PART

We have finished our journey together through the Stages of the Soul, the five "loves" we experience that begin with the First Love of conversion and culminate in Intimate Love—maturity and union with God. At each stage of the soul, we have seen the grand invitation from God to journey with Him, to grow and mature us in His love, and to radiate that love to whomever we meet.

No matter the stage we are in, a challenge lies before each of us: Are we willing to accept His invitation to the next stage? For readers of this book, the more immediate question is: What will you do with the knowledge you have gained here? The temptation may be to acquire more information on the spiritual journey but not allow it to actually inspire us toward change. Everything we learn in the spiritual life, we must—by His grace—put into action.

The dilemma is that many of us will choose not to put what we know into practice. The Barna Group, in its "2016 State of the Church" report, indicated that while 73 percent of Americans self-identify as Christian, only 35 percent had attended church in the past week and only 34 percent read the Bible on their own.[1] Not surprisingly then, the Body of Christ (for the most part) is made up of people in earlier Stages of the Soul. And while "there is rejoicing in the presence of the angels of God over one sinner who repents" (Luke 15:10), the likelihood is that few Christians will reach Stage Four and even fewer Stage Five. The reality is that most believers remain in either Stage Two or Three—either priding themselves in being good rule followers in Stage Two or, in Stage Three, losing themselves in nurturing their "false selves" through self-righteousness instead of who they are in Christ.

In fact, Stage Three often lasts for a couple decades or more . . . sometimes our entire lives. We become sidetracked by success, pleasure, and even "religious" activity. Our capacity to be deeply changed by Christ is numbed by mediocrity and apathy. Like Jacob, we wrestle with God rather than surrender the things that we hold onto tightly and that take the place of Him. We then are no longer captivated by the magnificence of Christ alone.

But our infinite God continues to work in our lives and never ceases to encourage us to experience more of Himself. From a human perspective, it is difficult to measure the trajectory of our growth. As mentioned in an earlier chapter, our path is not so much linear as it is a spiral—an ever-deepening surrender to and love of God. When necessary, as we advance to a new stage, we may find ourselves doubling back to the lessons in an earlier stage and gaining a far better understanding. For example, in Stage Three, as we struggle with our personal idols, we may find the need to return to the same hunger to learn that we had in Stage Two and delve into the study of Scripture in order to realign our hearts with God's heart. On this journey with God, nothing is wasted for our redemption and preparation for eternity.

In a world bound by space and time, the notion of eternity is hard to grasp. The messages the world would like us to believe say that if we eat the right food, make the right financial decisions, and check off our list of Christian activities, we will indeed live a long and fruitful life. But the truth is, our lives are ultimately not our own, and we can't, of course, guarantee the length of our lives. A. W. Tozer describes our finite lives:

> The days of the years of our lives are few, and swifter than a weaver's shuttle. Life is a short and fevered rehearsal for a concert we cannot stay to give. Just when we appear to have attained some proficiency, we are forced to lay our instruments down. There is simply not time enough to think, to become, to perform what the constitution of our natures indicates we are capable of.[2]

For some of us, our lives may be shorter than others . . .

I had a student in one of my classes named Tom. On the very first day of class, I was struck by the level of this young man's maturity, his tender heart, and his authentic passion for living for Christ. When Tom would share something in class about Christ, his words seemed to infuse the whole classroom with light; his love for Christ was contagious. Following that semester, Tom went on a road trip to Colorado.

On the way, he was killed in a car accident. His brief life was cut short; he was only twenty-three years old. When I received the news, I was shocked and grieved over the loss of this precious young man. But then it dawned on me. His life was not cut short; no time had been wasted. Tom was already living in an eternal reality with Christ. Every time he had spoken to us, he was providing a glimpse of his deep love of Christ and the lavish love of God. His entrance into eternity was simply a continuation of the knowledge, understanding, and love of Christ he so enthusiastically had been sharing with us.

Stories like Tom's, and those of others in the stages beyond ours, should inspire us to journey deeper. We are all invited to learn to live into the eternal reality of Christ and allow Him to shape us into people who are His representatives on earth. We are to be people who know, in every cell of our bodies, God's love for us and who are willing to show that to the world.

We live in sobering times. The forces of hate, polarization, and discord are mounting. Those who claim to be followers of Jesus Christ can no longer live their lives as chameleons, blending in with the culture. We can no longer live with *ourselves* as the axis by which our world turns. The radical call of Jesus Christ means our lives must be completely transformed. We can no longer love Christ with reservation. Being a follower of Christ can no longer be a badge we wear identifying ourselves as a political group. Nor can churches function as a country club with a "members only" sign posted out front. Our work and service for Christ can no longer be more important than our love and devotion *for* Christ. Our faith can no longer be primarily driven by our mastery of the Scriptures, our identification with an organization, or our loyalty to our leaders. We must be known for a love wrapped in mercy. In our lives, Christ must remain preeminent.

For some, especially those of us in Stages One, Two, or Three, this will mean we have to make difficult decisions as to where our loyalties lie. Jesus was clear with those choosing to follow Him: "No man who puts a hand to the plow and looks back is fit for service in the kingdom of heaven" (Luke 9:62). In addition, "If anyone comes to me and does not hate father and mother, wife and children, brothers and sisters—yes, even their own life—such a person cannot be my disciple" (Luke 14:26).

It is a serious business to say yes to Christ. We are called to forsake everything that is in the way of an undivided devotion to Christ. In what areas of our lives do we find our loyalties competing with Christ's lordship? Where do we settle for safety and comfort rather than sacrifice and service? The same question Jesus asked the apostle Peter, He poses continuously to us: "Who do you say I am?" (Matt. 16:15). He is not asking for intellectual assent but belief from the deep place of knowing in our hearts. Is Christ merely a teacher that gives us guidelines for effective living? Is He only a companion that soothes our anxieties? Or is He a lover who captivates our hearts? How we answer will determine the trajectory of our following Christ, especially in the early stages.

The deeper the spiraling path takes us on this journey

of our souls, the more Christ requires of us. Of course, we always have the option to refuse His invitations. The Scriptures tell us that as Jesus' teachings became costlier, many turned back and chose not to continue to follow Him (see John 6:66). For those, Jesus has stern warnings, such as those in His letters to the churches in the book of Revelation.

Jesus gave a sobering exhortation to the church of Laodicea in which He identified that they were neither hot nor cold but rather lukewarm (Rev. 3:15); they had acquired wealth and had no need. They were materially rich but spiritually poor (v. 17). They failed to recognize that their comfort, resources, and worldly acumen had replaced their zeal for Christ. The sin of their self-sufficiency and self-deceit had burrowed itself so deeply in their souls that, not only were they unaware of the sin, it was destroying them. They had replaced the power of God with their own competency and the reign of God with their own guidelines for living. In spite of their indifference, God was still reaching out to them in love and inviting them to draw near to Him. He loved them too much to allow them to remain where they were.

Christ will never allow anything to surpass His sovereign rule over our lives. "The love of God is not a mild benevolence; it is a consuming fire," states Bede Griffiths.[3] As with the church of Laodicea, He invites us to repent and turn from our self-reliant ways. We must humbly examine our souls on a daily basis to see if we are relying on ourselves or trusting in God's sufficiency. He promises that someday, if we remain faithful, we will sit down with Him at His throne and reign with Him (Rev. 3:21).

In my own life, I look back over the last twenty-five years and see God has been merciful in continuing to allow painful circumstances beyond my control to keep me awakened to His sufficiency and love. Reflecting on this, I see how quickly I have turned from Christ and His love rather than trusting even more in His good provision and care. He has been faithful in showing me the depths of my own narcissism, self-deceit, and brokenness. I am forever grateful that God has not left me to my own propensity to walk apart from Him. Without seeing the wickedness that dwells within me, I would never have grasped for the grace extended to me by His death on the cross. He has broken, and continues to break, the grip of my sin and the damage of sin committed by others.

He has, at pivotal turning points, posed to me, as He did to the apostle Peter, "Do you love me more than these?" I would like to say that my response has been, "Oh, yes, Lord, I do love you more than these." Rather, it has often been a struggle to finally relinquish to His grace. What I know now, more than ever before, is He indeed loves me ... and continues to invite me to deeper intimacy. This is the invitation of our lover, friend, and beloved Rabbi.

Thomas à Kempis, the author of *The Imitation of Christ*, speaks to the message throughout our journey of the Stages of the Soul. He writes:

> Hold fast to Jesus, both in life and death, and trust yourself to His faithfulness, for He alone can aid you when all others fail. Your Beloved is of such a nature that He will not share your love with another: He desires your heart for Himself alone,

and to reign there as a King on His throne. If you could empty your heart of all creatures, Jesus would delight to dwell with you. . . . Whatever trust you place in men rather than in Jesus is almost wholly wasted. Do not trust or lean on a windblown reed . . . for "all flesh is as grass, and its glory will fall like the flower of the grass."[4]

May we press on, "lay[ing] aside every weight, and sin which clings so closely" (Heb. 12:1 ESV), so that our "faith— of greater worth than gold, which perishes even though refined by fire—may result in praise, glory and honor when Jesus Christ is revealed" (1 Peter 1:7). May we let nothing dissuade us from the magnificent journey of God's invitation to the greatest love.

An example of a man who powerfully lived out what it means to press on in this journey was Angus McGillivray profiled in the book *Through the Valley of the Kwai* by Ernest Gordon about life in a World War II Japanese prison camp.

> Angus was a strong, brawny Scottish prisoner in the prisoner of war camp. The camp had deteriorated into a demoralizing place. Men lived by the rule of the jungle—survival of the fittest. Acts of meanness and suspicion were the order of the day. Men were stealing from and cheating each other. . . .
>
> It was custom for the Scottish soldiers to have a "mucker," a friend with whom he shared or "mucked in" everything he had. It was becoming evident to everyone that Angus's mucker was slowly dying. Everyone had given up on him—except for Angus. . . . At mealtimes Angus would get rations and take them to his mucker, stand over him, and force him to eat. Going hungry was difficult for Angus because he was a man with such a big frame. Angus did everything in his power to see that his buddy survived. In time Angus's mucker got better.

Then one day, Angus collapsed, slumped over, and died. When the doctors examined him, they discovered he had died of starvation complicated by exhaustion. Angus had been giving of his own food, shelter, and energy to his beloved mucker. He had given everything for him—to the point of his very own life.

As word spread of what Angus McGillivray had done, the atmosphere of the camp began to change. His sacrificial actions had given the men an inspiration of how they were to live. Men began to focus not only on helping each other but sacrificing for each other as well. They shared their talents with each other. A cobbler and an engineer together created an artificial leg for amputees. One prisoner was a violinmaker, another an orchestra leader. Within time the camp had an orchestra full of homemade instruments. The men started gatherings where they could teach each other history, philosophy, and mathematics. A library was formed where they would make known to each other the books they had and arranged by word of mouth to pass them to others. A church was formed, named the "Church Without Walls," that was so powerful, so compelling, that a spirit of worship pervaded the camp. The prisoner of war camp that once was a place of dehumanizing depravity became a place that was transformed into a sanctuary of love—all because one man named Angus gave all he had for love.[5]

"Greater love has no one than this: to lay down one's life for one's friends," Jesus said (John 15:13). What would compel Angus to give his life away for the sake of his friend? We believe Angus had a taste of eternity that blew apart all of his earthly fears of his own survival—and Angus left a taste of heaven to each of his fellow prisoners in the camp.

As you finish this book and continue your journey with

your Rabbi, my prayer for you echoes Paul's words from his letter to the Colossians, so I continually ask God . . .

> . . . to fill you with the knowledge of his will through all the wisdom and understanding that the Spirit gives, so that you may live a life worthy of the Lord and please him in every way: bearing fruit in every good work, growing in the knowledge of God, being strengthened with all power according to his glorious might so that you may have great endurance and patience, and giving joyful thanks to the Father, who has qualified you to share in the inheritance of his holy people in the kingdom of light. (Col. 1:9–12)

EPILOGUE

What's Next? Soul Stages
Journey in the Church

For many of you completing this *Stages of the Soul* book journey—inspired to assess where you are and to grow deeper in your love of God—you may be asking, "How do I translate what I've learned in the context of my church community?" This is a question that I'm regularly asked by students in my spiritual formation classes. Because of the change in perspective—and more importantly, in their walk with Christ—that they experience, they then desire to share this path with their church family as well.

Often, students begin the spiritual formation cohort thinking it will be another "class" about the Christian faith; but shortly into the process, they sense God shining His light on their souls in such a way they are actually encountering God in a deeper way. Eventually they are eager to bring what they've learned to their church but may find a less than enthusiastic reception from leadership.

Many churches, especially in a climate where so many people are leaving the church, lead from a Stage Two approach in which learning (Bible study) and doing (church activities), while good and valuable, are usually emphasized over "becoming." Activity in the church is given precedence over spiritual growth, and there can be a failure to recognize that maturity is not determined by one's activities but rather an ever-deepening relationship with Jesus Christ.[1]

So what are we to do? I have often said that as we understand this process of spiritual growth, God entrusts us to go back into the environments He has placed us in to live and teach others the way of intimacy with Christ. As has always been true for the advancement of the kingdom of God, it goes forward one individual at a time.

Especially impactful is when a pastor catches a vision of this soul stages process and invites church members into that process.

Rick was the pastor of a large, thriving church. At one point, as he led the church through a building campaign, a division arose among the elders as to the viability of the extent of the development. Some were afraid the building proposal was too large for the church to assume; others felt it was a necessary step for a thriving church. Still others felt the undertaking showed poor stewardship of funds when so much need already existed in the surrounding community. Members quickly chose sides. The conflict became so toxic that people started leaving the church and attendance plummeted to half. Rick was crestfallen. Sunday morning was an empty shell of what had once been.

Rick sought God in extended times of prayer as to what to do. Up until that point, he had been living and leading in Stage Two, primarily defining himself by his performance as a pastor. He was constantly pushing for more programs that offered church members a variety of ways to be involved. Through the pain of the church split, God was inviting Rick to see the pride he felt in leading a large and "successful" congregation.

God was ushering Rick into Stage Three by revealing to him how much of his own ego had been involved in leading the church. God also showed Rick how his pride was causing an emotional distance between him and his congregation, preventing Rick from loving the people in his church well. God showed him that his lack of becoming the leader/pastor the church needed was the primary reason for the division. Rick had been refusing God's invitations to step into the conflict and become, like Christ, someone who actually enters into others' pain as a reconciler.

Finally, Rick met with each person on the board, as well as key families who had left the church. He listened to their fears, hurts, and anger. He vulnerably confessed his failure to become the shepherd they needed. As a result of witnessing their pastor's confession and vulnerability, people started seeking each other out to reconcile. Ultimately, all but a few of the original members reconciled and returned to the church.

Rick invited the church into Stage Three living. He started teaching about the need to slow their lives down and seek God in extended prayer. He started teaching about what it means to live in the fullness of God's love moment by moment. His sermons became more confessionary as to the struggles he was encountering and then testifying to how God was meeting him in those places. Board meetings became marked by vulnerable prayer and people admitting their failures and sin before entering into discussion of the business at hand. The meetings were marked by acceptance and compassion. The church started recovery groups. It was remarkable to see how Rick's movement into his soul's journey became a catalyst for the rest of the church to grow in its love for God and one another.

How can a church practically implement what we have learned about the stages of the soul's growth? In an ideal world, the church would have a solid understanding of the process of spiritual growth and the stages involved. The church would reflect believers at each stage of the soul's journey, and those believers would minister to each other. Believers in Stage One—First Love would remind those in the later stages of the joy of the new birth. The church would be mindful to tenderly shepherd those in Stage Two with the necessary fundamentals of the faith. Those in Stage Three would have a place to ask questions and explore seasons of doubt and pain that arise in this stage. Those in the latter stages of Stage Four would bring time-tested wisdom and assurance of God's provision in the face of anxiety. Those in the last stage would be an inspiration to the other believers of what life with Christ can become.

Believers in every stage would be singularly focused on Christ. There would be a common seeking to understand and grow with each other with no animosity or competitiveness shown toward people in other stages. An environment of empathy, openness, and acceptance would make people feel at home, no matter their stage. Women and men would share an equal voice in dialogue; people would not be segregated by ethnicity or social status. The homeless would be welcomed and not seen as a "mission opportunity." Children would be woven into the fabric of gatherings. There would be a heart of service, not marked by activism but fueled by compassion. Materialism and prosperity would be replaced with simplicity and radical generosity. There would be a sense of being known and fully accepted.

While we cannot prescribe a church to move through the stages of spiritual growth, we can encourage a culture and ethos within the church that would provide ground in which spiritual growth could thrive. The following qualities, if nurtured within the Body of Christ, can provide the necessary conditions for the stages of each believer's soul to mature.

BROKEN AND SURRENDERED

The fellowship of God's people will recognize on a daily basis that without Christ, they are powerless to make good from their lives. We are all shipwrecked and broken on the reef of life's shores, whether we choose to recognize it or not. Coming to the end of ourselves is the only way to realize God's redemption and healing. Death to self is the only way to life. Jesus reminds us that, "Unless a kernel of wheat falls to the ground and dies, it remains only a single seed. But if it dies, it produces many seeds" (John 12:24).

This is no small thing. W. H. Auden writes,

> We would rather be ruined than changed,
> We would rather die in our dread

Than climb the cross of the moment
And let our illusions die.[2]

We must unlearn our way of living to receive and live into the kingdom of heaven. It cannot be achieved by trying to change one's behavior while not addressing the inward issues of the heart. Nor can it be done believing we can somehow make ourselves "good." This can only be done by the Spirit of God.

SELF-REFLECTION AND SOUL EXAMINATION

It has been said that "Evil proceeds from a lack of consciousness."[3] It is imperative, therefore, that God's people must daily examine their souls before God, seeking Him to identify where they have lived in their own merits and false self and when they have seen God's gracious provision. This is not a self-introspective critical analysis but bringing ourselves before the presence of God asking Him to shine His light on our souls (Ps. 139:23–24). Consequently, confession becomes a normal daily part of the walk with Christ, not the exception. This practice assists us in sustaining a humble heart before God and facilitates a follower who is readily kind, gracious, and merciful to others.

FORGIVEN AND FORGIVE

"But God demonstrates his own love for us in this: While we were still sinners, Christ died for us" (Rom. 5:8). It is God's love for us, when we were and are in sin, that invites us to repentance and transformation. Indeed, "love covers a multitude of sins" (1 Peter 4:8 ESV). Sin and failure are the opportunity for the redemption of God. Jesus said that those who are forgiven much love much (Luke 7:46–47). The fellowship of God's people are to be known by their willingness to confess, forgive, and be forgiven just as God forgave them.

TRANSPARENT

"If we walk in the light, as he is in the light, we have fellowship with one another, and the blood of Jesus his Son cleanses us from all sin" (1 John 1:7 ESV). The fellowship of God's people are able to be appropriately transparent with each other and celebrate in the sustaining grace of Christ to strengthen us. As we walk in the light, we increasingly live a life without masks and distortions. "In their relations to others, they are completely transparent. Because they walk in goodness they have no use for darkness, and they achieve real contact or fellowship with others," explains Dallas Willard.[4]

ACCEPTING—NON-JUDGMENTAL

Because we are vividly aware of our own sin, we are able to extend mercy to others. We all stand equally before the cross of Christ. No one is more advanced than others in the kingdom of heaven—we are equally God's children. At any moment, we are all capable of sin. Therefore, we are not surprised by the failings of others, but rather extend the love and mercy of God when others stumble and fall.

GRATEFUL

We recognize that everything we have and are, every breath we take, are gifts from God. As we grow, we will realize ever deeper levels of gratitude and awareness that the whole world is infused with the presence and glory of God (Heb. 1:3a). Our eyes will ever be turned to see the face of God. We will look for Him in others, in nature, and in the moments of solitude. "Because [the face of God] is so lovely, my brothers and sisters," Augustine says, "so beautiful, that once you have seen it, nothing else can give you pleasure. It will give insatiable satisfaction of which we will never tire. We shall always be hungry and always have our fill."[5]

COMPASSIONATE

As followers of Christ, we will comfort others with the same comfort we have received from God (2 Cor. 1:3–5). The root of compassion is "com" (with), "patior" (suffer)—to suffer with. We are willing to extend ourselves and to suffer with others in their hurt when we know and recognize how much we have needed others in our own times of pain.

TRANSFORMATIONAL

As followers of Christ, we will daily surrender ourselves in obedience to God and the mandates of Scripture. We will learn how to live the values of the kingdom of God in every aspect of our lives resulting in concrete, tangible change.

RHYTHM (SPIRITUAL PRACTICES)

In our attention to follow Christ and be open to all He has to teach us, we will implement a daily rhythm of prayer and spiritual practices that assist us in opening our souls for God to work. This may include the traditionally observed spiritual practices of fasting, Bible study, simplicity, times of solitude, service, submission, confession, guidance, celebration, and worship.

LIFE-GIVING

The fellowship of God's people, as they grow and become formed more and more into His likeness, will bring the redemptive life of Christ wherever they are. They will place a high value on relationships seeking to honor others above themselves (Rom. 12:9–10). They will honor God's creation by cooperating with the earth's restoration and preservation. They will value all that is good, true, and beautiful in the world and seek to bring forth God's goodness in the world.

As you may notice, these qualities are listed in sequence. In summary, we recognize we are all *broken* and *surrender* to become who God calls us to be through the process of *self-reflection* and *soul examination*. As we more deeply understand that our sins have been *forgiven,* we can then more freely *forgive* others. Therefore, our ability to become more authentic and *transparent* increases. As a result, our soul's capacity to become more *accepting* and nonjudgmental enables us to become *grateful,* enabling us to become focused and energized as to allow the presence and majesty of God to change and *transform* us.

As we grow in both our love toward God and for others, we begin to see ourselves more and more reflecting the character of Christ. We find that we are eager to implement a daily *rhythm* of prayer and spiritual practices into our lives to open our souls for God to work. We then, from the abundance of what God has given us, are *life giving* people, overflowing with goodness and life to the world around us.

May the following prayer from *The Book of Common Prayer* be the desire for all of God's people as we allow God to mature us:

> Almighty God, you have built your Church upon the foundation of the apostles and prophets, Jesus Christ himself being the chief cornerstone: Grant us so to be joined together in unity of spirit by their teaching, that we may be made a holy temple acceptable to you; through Jesus Christ our Lord, who lives and reigns with you and the Holy Spirit, one God, for ever and ever. Amen.[6]

ACKNOWLEDGMENTS

Developing and then writing *Stages of the Soul* could not have been accomplished without a cast of characters by my side. There are so many people to whom I am indebted—for their love and unwavering belief that this book could be written.

First, I'd like to thank my husband, Ray. If it wasn't for his belief in me to step out and take risks in love and life, who knows where I would have ended up. His tireless affection and patience have been daily reminders of God's tender love. Each chapter of our life together gets richer than the one before. I love him more than I can put into words, and I treasure each day we get to do life together.

My beloved Kane family—Eric Kane, Krista Kane-Witzig, and Jeff Kane-Witzig—you have brought laughter and immeasurable joy to my heart. You are each "wise beyond your years" and kept my feet firmly planted on the ground as I wrote this book. I am so grateful we are on this crazy ride together called "life."

Bob Sears's fingerprints of love, grace, hope, peace, wisdom, and discernment are forever woven into the message of this book and my life. He has been the person who has brought together, in my darkest time, the shattered puzzle pieces of my life to make a whole picture. From our first meeting, he has pointed me to the process of growing in Christ and encouraging me to live every moment with Christ and eternity in sight. I highly recommend Bob's work on spiritual formation and his enlightening article "Healing and Family Spiritual/Emotional Systems" in the *Journal of Christian Healing*.

Duane Sherman exhibited an incredible ability to bring forward a concise and relevant message in this book, drawing from the passion in my heart to the random minutiae of information in my head. His giftedness is only exceeded by his exemplary character. If only the world were populated with more people like Duane.

Amanda Cleary Eastep brought needed laughter and tender compassion while making the painful but necessary edits to the manuscript. She has the giftedness of a master surgeon, knowing where to cut and how to help shape the core message of this book.

Nadine Rorem has been a friend in the true sense of the word. With prayer, compassion, and the uncanny ability to see right through situations, she has kept me on the straight and narrow path of seeing the truth about myself and others.

Jenny Haas has consistently lifted my weary arms of faith. At pivotal points, her discerning heart and faithful prayers have been just what I needed to strengthen my faith and see Christ more clearly.

Dan Allender took time to read the manuscript when it was in its rawest form and provided much needed encouragement. His passion for inviting people to truth in the deepest parts of our souls continues to be a source of constant inspiration.

So many have been faithfully praying for me and this book, including: Carol Reed, Lois Tawfik, Christopher Suder, Ingmari Wahlgren, Ruth Singleton, Veronica Peppers, Ava Perry, Cheryl Fulton, Cathy Clarke, Lorri Larson, and Donna Cooper. I have been immensely moved by their commitment to pray and their encouragement behind this work.

SOLI DEO GLORIA

NOTES

Introduction

1. Ed Stetzer, "The State of The Church in America: When Numbers Point To A New Reality, Part 1," *Christianity Today*, September 12, 2016, https://www.christianitytoday.com/edstetzer/2016/september/state-of-american-church-when-numbers-point-to-new-reality.html.
2. For more information on the Pew study, visit: http://www.pewresearch.org/fact-tank/2015/05/12/5-key-findings-u-s-religious-landscape/.
3. Stetzer, "The State of The Church in America."
4. A. W. Tozer, *The Pursuit of God* (Chicago: Moody, 2015), 42–43.
5. Many similar definitions exist, but this is the definition I have written for use in my classes.
6. Thomas Aquinas noted these in *Summa Theologica*, "Man's Last End 2(a) Where Happiness Can Be Found."
7. Bertrand Russell, *The Selected Letters of Bertrand Russell, Volume 1: The Public Years*, 1914–1970 (New York: Routledge, 2002), https://books.google.com/books, 49.
8. C. S. Lewis, *The Problem of Pain* (1940; repr., New York: HarperOne, 2001), 91.

Chapter 1: Growing Toward Wholeness, Holiness, and Love— A Reliable Map

1. Joseph Campbell, *A Joseph Campbell Companion: Reflections on the Art of Living* (San Anselmo, CA: Joseph Campbell Foundation, 2011).
2. C. S. Lewis, *Mere Christianity* (1952; repr., New York: HarperOne, 2001), 205.
3. Kevin D. Zuber, "Luke," in *The Moody Bible Commentary*, Michael Rydelnik and Michael Vanlaningham, eds. (Chicago: Moody, 2014), 1596.
4. Mrs. Howard Taylor, *Borden of Yale '09* (Philadelphia: China Inland Mission, 1926).
5. Jayson Casper, "The Forgotten Final Resting Place of William Borden," *Christianity Today*, https://www.christianitytoday.com/history/2017/february/forgotten-final-resting-place-of-william-borden.html.
6. "The Philanthropists: William Borden, Challies.com, November 3, 2013, https://www.challies.com/articles/the-philanthropists-william-borden.
7. Joseph William Cochran, *William Borden of Yale, The Man with a Million for the Kingdom* (Philadelphia: Westminster Press, 1917), Kindle edition.

8. Find A Grave (website), https://www.findagrave.com/memorial /15641525/william-whiting-borden.

Chapter 2: Stage One: Our First Love—Called into Saving Faith

1. Francis Thompson, *The Hound of Heaven* (Portland, ME: Thomas Bird Mosher, 1908).
2. Henri Nouwen, lecture delivered at Scarrett-Bennett Center, Nashville, Tennessee, February 8, 1991.
3. Tim Keller, *Encounters with Jesus: Unexpected Answers to Life's Biggest Questions* (New York: Penguin Books), 35.
4. Augustine, *The Confessions of St. Augustine*, https://www.goodreads .com/quotes/669135-late-have-i-loved-you-o-beauty-ever-ancient- ever. For the original version in Augustine's Tenth Book, 38, see *The Confessions of St. Augustine*, Rosalie De Rosset, gen. ed. (Chicago: Moody, 2007), 273.
5. C. S. Lewis, *The Problem of Pain* (1940; repr., New York: HarperOne, 2001), 152.
6. Sheila Fabricant Linn, Dennis Linn, and Matthew Linn, *Healing Our Beginning* (Mahwah, NJ: Paulist Press, 2005), 21.
7. A. W. Tozer, *The Knowledge of the Holy* (New York: HarperOne, 1961), 29.
8. Kevin D. Zuber, "Luke," in *The Moody Bible Commentary*, Michael Rydelnik and Michael Vanlaningham, eds. (Chicago: Moody, 2014), 1475.
9. Tim Keller, *Walking With God through Pain and Suffering* (New York: Riverhead Books, 2013), 47.

Chapter 3: Stage Two: Obedient Love—Learning the Ways of Godliness

1. David G. Myers, "Resolving the American Paradox," David G. Myers (website), reprinted from *USA Today* online edition, June 29, 2000, http://www.davidmyers.org/Brix?pageID=68.
2. Colin Smith, "How the Order of the Beatitudes Could Change Your Life," The Gospel Coalition, February 10, 2017, https:// www.thegospelcoalition.org/article/how-order-of-beatitudes- could-change-your-life.
3. The Forerunner Commentary, https://www.bibletools.org/index .cfm/fuseaction/Topical.show/RTD/cgg/ID/4260/Makarios.htm.
4. https://www.studylight.org/language-studies/greek-thoughts .html?article=11.
5. Ibid.
6. Matthew Henry's Commentary (concise), https://www.christianity .com/bible/commentary.php?com=mhc&b=40&c=5.
7. https://www.biblestudytools.com/dictionary/meekness.
8. http://www.edgewaterhistory.org/ehs/treasures/2014c.
9. Arloa Sutter, *The Invisible: What the Church Can Do to Find and Serve the Least of These*, Kindle edition, 64.

10. Ibid.

Chapter 4: Stage Three: Persevering Love—Invitation to Intimacy

1. Donald Miller, "The Gospel of Jesus, More Like Marriage, Less Like Formula," Seattle Pacific University, Speakers & Events, November 30, 2005, https://digitalcommons.spu.edu /av_events/878/.

2. John Ortberg, *Soul Keeping* (Grand Rapids: Zondervan 2014), Kindle edition, 182.

3. As quoted in "Stroke of Grace," Gary Black Jr., *Conversations Journal*, Fall/Winter 2013.

4. Craig Borlase, "Meet Dieter Zander . . . The Living Parable of the Modern-Day Worship Leader?", November 5, 2014, https://www .weareworship.com/us/blog/meet-dieter-zander/Posted.

5. Ibid.

6. Trevor Hudson, *Christ-Following: Ten Signposts to Spirituality*, as referenced in *Surrender to Love: Discovering the Heart of Christian Spirituality* (Downers Grove, IL: InterVarsity Press, 2003), 81.

7. Thomas Merton, *New Seeds of Contemplation* (New York: New Directions Paperbook, 1972), 34-35.

8. James Finley, *Merton's Place of Nowhere* (Notre Dame: AveMarie Press, 2017), 4.

9. M. Robert Mulholland Jr., *The Deeper Journey: The Spirituality of Discovering Your True Self* (Downers Grove, IL: InterVarsity Press, 2016).

10. Term coined by Frederich Buechner.

11. David Benner, *The Gift of Being Yourself* (Downers Grove, IL: Inter-Varsity Press, 2004), 102.

12. Richard Rohr, *Falling Upward—A Spirituality of the Two Halves of Life* (San Francisco: Wiley Imprint Jossey-Bass, 2011), 51.

13. For an excellent study of this, I recommend Tim Keller's book *Counterfeit Gods—The Empty Promises of Money, Sex and Power and the Only Hope That Matters*.

14. R. C. Sproul, *Surprised by Suffering: The Role of Pain and Death in The Christian Life* (Wheaton, IL: Tyndale House, 1988), 77.

15. Brennan Manning, *The Furious Longing of God* (Colorado Springs, CO: David C. Cook, 2009), 55–56.

Chapter 5: Stage Four: Sacrificial Love—Living the Kingdom Here and Now

1. Robertson McQuilkin, "Living by the Vows" testimony was pub-lished in *Christianity Today* in 1990 and was then printed as a free pamphlet by Columbia International University.

2. Ibid.

3. Gerald Peterman, "Ephesians," in *The Moody Bible Commentary*, Michael Rydelnik and Michael Vanlaningham, eds. (Chicago: Moody, 2014), 1851.

4. Tozer, *The Pursuit of God*, (Chicago: Moody, 2015), 296–97.

5. Thomas Merton, *Contemplation in a World of Action* (Garden City, NY: Doubleday Image Book, 1973), 175.

6. Francois Fenelon, *Spiritual Letters of Archbishop Fénelon: Letters to Women*, Kindle edition, 320.

7. Benedict J. Groeschel, *Spiritual Passages—The Psychology of Spiritual Development* (New York: The Crossroad Publishing Company, 1999). Page 145 speaks of the gifts of virtue that one receives in the illuminative stage.

8. Malcolm Muggeridge, *Jesus Rediscovered* (New York: Doubleday, 1979), 47–48.

9. For more of Mama Maggie's story, read *Mama Maggie: The Untold Story of One Woman's Mission to Love the Forgotten Children of Egypt's Garbage Slums* by Martin Makary (Nashville: Thomas Nelson Publishers, 2015).

10. Quote from her speech at Willow Creek Leadership Summit, August 11, 2011.

11. http://www.stephenschildren.org/about.

12. Groeschel, *Spiritual Passages*, 153. He writes about the danger of spiritual "greed" and self-righteousness and a feeling of being elected to a special mission.

13. Ibid, 154–55.

14. Friedrich Nietzsche, *Beyond Good and Evil: Prelude to a Philosophy of the Future*, Jan Oliveira, ed., translated by Helen Zimmern (Rastro Digital, September 5, 2015), Kindle edition, 62.

15. Selwyn Hughes, "What Movement Toward God Looks Like," *Conversations Journal—A Forum for Authentic Transformation*, Vol 2:2 Fall 2004, 8.

16. Ibid.

17. Robertson McQuilkin, *A Promise Kept – The Story of Unforgettable Love* (Wheaton, IL: Tyndale House Publishers, 1998), 32–33.

18. St. Francis's prayer:
For it is in giving that we receive;
It is in pardoning that we are pardoned;
And it is in dying that we are born to eternal life.

Chapter 6: Stage Five: Intimate Love—Being Light and Love for the World

1. Shel Silverstein, *The Giving Tree* (New York: HarperCollins, 1962).

2. C. S. Lewis, *Mere Christianity* (1952; repr., New York: HarperOne, 2001), 205–6.

3. It is important to note that as long as we are in our body of flesh, we will be vulnerable to sin. In this stage, we are free from a willful choice to turn away from God.

4. Paul A. Wright, *Mother Teresa's Prescription—Finding Happiness and Peace in Service* (Nortre Dame, IN: Ave Maria Press, 2006), 87.

5. Bruce Demarest, *Seasons of the Souls—Stages of Spiritual Development* (Downers Grove, IL: InterVarsity Press, 2009), 132.

6. For more on Dallas Willard's life from those who knew him, go to: *Eternal Living: Reflections on Dallas Willard's Teachings on Faith and Formation*, Gary Moon, (Downers Grove, IL: InterVarsity Press, 2015).

7. Gary W. Moon, *Becoming Dallas Willard: The Formation of a Philosopher, Teacher, and Christ Follower* (Downers Grove, IL: InterVarsity Press, 2018), Kindle edition, 251.

8. Kate Shellnutt, "What it was like to be Billy Graham's Pastor," *Christianity Today*, February 23, 2018, https://www.christianitytoday.com/ct/2018/february-web-only/billy-graham-pastor-don-wilton-funeral-interview.html.

9. Gordon Fee, *Paul's Letter to the Philippians* (Grand Rapids: Eerdman's Publishing, 1995), as referenced in https://gentle reformation.com/2015/03/10/sharing-in-the-suffering-of-christ.

10. United States Commission on International Religious Freedom, Annual Report 2015, Washington, DC, https://www.uscirf.gov/sites/default/files/USCIRF%20Annual%20Report%202015%20(2).pdf, page 2.

11. Bob Fu, "Religious Freedom, Human Rights, and Rule of Law Deteriorating Rapidly in China," Congressional-Executive Commission on China, July 23, 2015, https://www.cecc.gov/sites/chinacommission.house.gov/files/CECC%20Hearing%20-%20Religious%20Freedom%20-%2023July15%20-%20Bob%20Fu.pdf, page 2.

12. A. W. Tozer, *The Root of the Righteous* (Chicago: Moody, 1986), 160.

13. May Quinlan, *Damien of Molokai* (London: R. & T. Washbourne, Ltd., 1914), Kindle edition.

14. "Heroes of the Faith: Father Damien," May 21, 2015, https://www.evangelicalsforsocialaction.org/heroes-of-the-faith/heroes-of-the-faith-father-damien.

15. Ted Olsen, "'We Lepers,'" *Christianity Today*, September 17, 2009, https://www.christianitytoday.com/history/2009/september/we-lepers.html.

16. Quinlan, *Damien of Molokai*.

Chapter 7: Before We Part

1. "The State of the Church 2016," September 15, 2016, https://www.barna.com/research/state-church-2016.

2. Tozer, *Knowledge of the Holy*, 52.

3. Bede Griffiths, as quoted in Brennan Manning, *The Relentless Tenderness of Jesus* (Grand Rapids: Revell, 2004), 111.

4. Thomas a Kempis, *The Inner Life*, translated by Leo Sherley-Price (New York: Penguin Books, 1952), 33.

5. Excerpt from Nancy and Ray Kane's book *From Fear to Love* (Chicago: Moody, 2002), 124–26.

Epilogue: What's Next? Soul Stages Journey in the Church

1. An excellent book on this topic is by Greg Hawkins and Cally Parkinson: *Move: What 1,000 Churches Reveal about Spiritual Growth*.

2. W. H. Auden, *The Age of Anxiety: A Baroque Eclogue*, Alan Jacobs, ed. (Princeton, NJ: Princeton University Press, 2011), 105.

3. Richard Rohr, *Breathing Under Water* (Cincinnati, OH: St. Anthony Messenger Press, 2011), 35.

4. Dallas Willard, *Renovation of the Heart* (Colorado Springs, CO: NavPress, 2002), 220.

5. Trevin Wax, "The Glory of God: Quotes," The Gospel Coalition, February 16, 2013, https://www.thegospelcoalition.org/blogs/trevin-wax/the-glory-of-god-quotes.

6. Proper 8 (the Sunday closest to June 29), *The Book of Common Prayer* (New York: Oxford University Press, 1979), 230.

APPENDIX A

Where Are You on the Soul Stages Journey?

In order to aid you in determining your areas of spiritual growth and the approximate stage you may be in, the following assessment tool details certain character traits commonly found in each of the soul stages. These traits are listed on a spectrum from the most negative aspect of the trait to the most positive: fear/love, doubt/trust, pride/humility, and sloth*/growth.

As you prayerfully reflect on the traits and their spectrums, circle the number that best represents where you believe yourself to be on the scale. If you already identify with a particular soul stage, this will help you identify areas of potential growth. If, after reading the book, you still aren't sure which stage you're currently in, honestly contemplating the various traits should help clarify this.

As we are complex people, you may find that you exhibit certain character traits from a different stage. For example, you may struggle with the kind of fear that is more common in Stage Two, while also trusting God in a way that is typical of someone in Stage Three.

---

* Spiritual "sloth" is indifference or lack of interest in spiritual practices such as prayer, reflection, and Bible reading. It is not laziness, but rather a lack of effort to seek God and His kingdom. Consequently, our work, our relationships, and our "doing" become more important than taking time to come into God's presence.

CHARACTER TRAIT	STAGE ONE FIRST LOVE	STAGE TWO OBEDIENT LOVE
FEAR	**1** The fear of God motivates me to consider Him.	**1** I fear the rejection and judgment of God and others causing me to focus more on my behavior than on a heart change.
LOVE	I love God because I have come to realize how much He loves me. **5**	My love for God motivates me to grow in understanding the precepts and truths of the faith. **5**
DOUBT	**1** I doubt whether I can trust God because I am used to running my own life.	**1** I doubt whether God can take care of my daily practical needs.
TRUST	I trust God with all of who I am for I understand His unconditional love for me. **5**	I trust God will give me a new heart to keep His commandments. **5**
PRIDE	**1** I tend to go back to taking control of my life and being my own "god."	**1** I live my life for the praise of others.
HUMILITY	My heart is open to relinquish all I am to all of who God is. **5**	I minister to others with a servant's heart. **5**
SPIRITUAL SLOTH	**1** I have little interest in seeking God.	**1** I become negligent in spiritual practices of Bible reading, prayer, and reflection.
SPIRITUAL GROWTH	I am enthusiastic about following Christ. **5**	I choose to grow because it is the right thing to do. **5**

148

STAGE THREE PERSEVERING LOVE	STAGE FOUR SACRIFICIAL LOVE	STAGE FIVE INTIMATE LOVE
1 I fear relinquishing control of the idols in my life and facing my own pride. My love for God flows from my desire to know Him and to grow deeper to reflect the character of Christ. **5**	**1** I consistently experience that God's unconditional love does melt away my fears allowing me to live more consistently in faith, hope, and love. My love for God is expressed through joyfully and sacrificially loving others. **5**	**1** Fear is simply a reminder to rest in God's love, grace, and forgiveness and to bask in His holy love and purpose for my life. My love for God has become an ever-present awareness of God's presence in me and with me. **5**
1 I doubt whether God really sees me and desires to know me in the most vulnerable places in my heart. I trust God to heal my deepest wounds. **5**	**1** I doubt the depth of my faith can sustain me in difficult times. I more fully trust God's abiding and loving presence in my life. **5**	**1** Having experienced God's love on such a deep level, I find my doubts quickly dissipate. I trust God fully and completely. **5**
1 I seek positions of importance in the spiritual life and mask by my pride with religious practices. I desire to serve and love others with greater purity. **5**	**1** I see myself as having achieved farther in the spiritual life than others. Because of God's mercy, I seek to extend His mercy to others. **5**	**1** I have a godly sorrow over the damage the sin of pride has done in my life and others. Humility is expressed by reconciling, serving, and loving all of God's children. **5**
1 I am unwilling to spend time in deeper reflection allowing God to shine His light on my heart. I choose to grow because I desire a more intimate relationship with God. **5**	**1** I move away from spiritual practices, replacing them with ministry and activity. I choose to grow in order to live in God's will, speak His truth, and share His heart of compassion for others. **5**	**1** Any temptation toward sloth is responded to immediately with confession. My will desires more than anything for my heart to beat with God's heart. **5**

It is important to remember that the point of our growth is not to "get" to another stage as much as it is to allow God to shine His light into areas of our souls that need to be transformed by Him. Our awareness of where we are in the journey must lead us to greater humility and dependence upon Him.

APPENDIX B

Various Models of the Stages of Faith

Numerous people over the centuries, from men and women of faith to secular psychologists, have explored the stages of faith development. While there is no "right" model, they all seek to inform us of the intricacies involved in the development of the journey toward maturity in Christ.

The model I propose synthesizes concepts found in a variety of models, while at the same time honoring the truths found in Scripture, as well as the stages of Christ's life. The overall focus of the model is God's invitation to greater intimacy and love.

The following chart identifies notable authors and models of stages of faith from the historic Christian church to the contemporary age.

	STAGE ONE	STAGE TWO
Nancy Kane **Stages of the Soul—God's Invitation to Greater Love**	Our First Love— *Called into Saving Faith*	Obedient Love— *Learning the Ways of Godliness*
James Fowler	Intuitive Projective Faith— Magical World	Mythic Literal Faith (Concrete Familial)
Evan Howard	First Year of Life— Crawling/Walking	Solid Growth as a Child of God—Stepping/Playing/Working
Janet Hagberg & Robert Guerlich	Salvation	Life of discipleship
Bernard of Clairvaux	Love of self for self- immature love	Love of God for self-prudent love
John Westerhoff	Experienced Faith	Affiliative Faith
St. John of the Cross	Conversion	Purgative Way
Teresa of Avila	First Dwelling: Spiritual Friendship	Second Dwelling: Prayers are brief service self-centered
Robert Sears	Initial Faith (Abrahamic Basic Trust)	Familial Faith (Mosaic Law)
Aaron Weisser	Encountering God's Spirit	Encountering God's Spirit in Me
Classic Orthodox	Awakening/Purgation	Ilumination
Walter Brueggemann	Securely oriented with God (Israel's deliverance from Egypt)	Painfully disoriented (Israel's wilderness wanderings)
Jan Van Ruysbroeck	Active life	IInterior life
Jane Loevinger	Conformist	Self-Aware
Evelyn Underhill	Awakening	Purification
Paula Rinehart	Predictability (Illusion)	Disillusionment (Disappointment)

STAGE THREE	STAGE FOUR	STAGE FIVE	STAGE SIX
Persevering Love— *Invitation to Intimacy*	Sacrificial Love— *Living the Kingdom Here and Now*	Intimate Love— *Being Light and Love for the World*	
Synthetic Conventional Faith	Individuative-Reflective Faith	Conjunctive Faith	Selfless Services
Thriving within Tension— Climbing/Dancing/Journeying	Living a Mature Christian Life—Active Resting		
The Productive Life	"The Wall" and The Journey Inward	The Journey Outward	The Life of Love
Love of God for God— unselfish love	Love of self for God—perfect love		
Searching Faith— late adolescence	Owned Faith		
Purifying Dark Night of the Senses	Illuminative Way	Dark Night of the Spirit	Unitive Way
Third Dwelling: Outward acts of compassion but lacks intimacy	Fourth Dwelling: Spiritual Courtship	Fifth Dwelling: Deep Communion with Christ	Sixth Dwelling: Spiritual Marriage
Individuating Faith (Jeremiah/Job)	Communitarian Faith (Jesus: Servant)	Mission Faith (Cross as God's Glory)	
Encountering God's Spirit in Others	Encountering God's Spirit in All		
Union			
Securely re-oriented (Israel's entry into Canaan)			
Contemplative life (deep union)	Missional Life		
Conscientious	Individualistic	Autonomous	
Illumination	Dark Night	Union with God	
Hope (Deepening Faith)			

MOODY DISTANCE LEARNING

Christian Spiritual Formation Certificate program

Join the Christian Spiritual Formation Certificate program, a one or two-year non-accredited cohort program designed to help you learn how to abide in Christ, to see your life and character transformed into a greater likeness of His image, and strengthen your walk with Him. You will also learn how to minister to others through spiritual formation and instruction in the church.

The program is divided into four weekend retreats throughout the year. Each retreat includes teaching, worship, shared meals together, times of reflection, spiritual direction groups, and personal meetings with a spiritual director. Encounter Christ in a new way as you grasp a deeper sense of the process of spiritual transformation, and meet Christ in community with others who want to deepen their relationship with Him.

Following each retreat is a 10–12 week curriculum that will wholistically engage you in discovering deeper intimacy with Christ.

For more information about the Christian Spiritual Formation Certificate program go to **MOODY.EDU/SPIRITUALFORMATION**

For more information about Nancy Kane and her husband's ministry go to **RAYNANCYKANE.COM**

MOODY
Bible Institute™
DISTANCE LEARNING

CHRISTIAN
SPIRITUAL
FORMATION
CERTIFICATE
PROGRAM

ARE YOU DISSATISFIED WITH YOUR SPIRITUAL LIFE?

A STORY OF TRAGEDY, TRUTH, AND REBELLIOUS HOPE

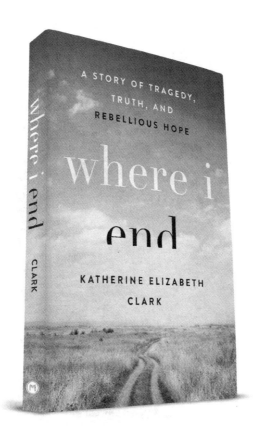

For fans of Ann Voskamp, Sheldon Vanauken, and Joni Eareckson Tada, *Where I End* tells the story of one woman's traumatic injury and God's incredible healing. In a reflective, literary style, Kate invites readers to see pain and suffering within the context of God's loving, tender, powerful care—and there find hope.

978-0-8024-1683-4   I   also available as an eBook

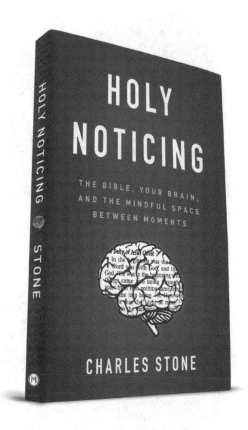